Early Endorsements for Baptism's Beauty and Benefits

Here is a book crammed with insights regarding the covenantal nature of baptism. Whether you come to this study as an immersionist or as one convinced of infant baptism, you will be persuaded by David to take a fresh look at the significance of this doctrine in the life of the church. Throughout the book as a whole, David calls upon the church to rise above the denominational discord surrounding Holy Baptism, and to be the church Jesus interceded for in John 17.

—**Philip Pidgeon**, DMin, EdD
Assistant Director for Research,
Clemson University Automotive Safety Research Institute

I highly commend Dr. David Rountree for his work in *Baptism's Beauty and Benefits*. Dr. Rountree is a successful pastor who has many years of experience in explaining baptism to his own congregants, as well as Christians from different doctrinal perspectives. His presentation of baptism is exceedingly practical, truly demonstrating *Baptism's Beauty and Benefits*. Baptism was ordained by our Lord Jesus Christ to mark out His people in the world. Unfortunately, too few Christians really comprehend baptism's meaning and purpose. Dr. Rountree has provided us with an extremely helpful and a much needed study of this glorious sacrament.

—**Rev. Kenneth L. Gentry**, Jr., ThD
Director of NiceneCouncil.com and
GoodBirth Ministries. Author, *Nourishment from the Word: Select Studies in Reformed Theology*, and over twenty other books.

David Rountree's book on baptism is rich with pastoral wisdom, pastoral tone, and pastoral experience. Even if you do not agree in every detail, this book explains baptism in very accessible terms. You can give this book to friends and relatives without fear that they will be ridiculed, caricatured, or treated disrespectfully. If we could all speak as *carefully* as David Rountree, then baptism would be more of the blessing to the church our Lord intends.

—**Bryan Chapell**, PhD
President of Covenant Theological Seminary

Baptism's Beauty *and* Benefits

Baptism's Beauty *and* Benefits

Emerging More Biblical and Blessed from the Comforting Waters of Baptism

David Rountree

WinePress Publishing (PO Box 428, Enumclaw, WA 98022) functions only as book publisher. As such, the ultimate design, content, editorial accuracy, and views expressed or implied in this work are those of the author.

ISBN 13: 978-1-4141-2098-0
ISBN 10: 1-4141-2098-2
Library of Congress Catalog Card Number: 2011928931

Contents

Introduction

DEBBIE WAS A member at our church for over ten years when marriage swept her away. Her husband's church demanded she be rebaptized as required by their local church membership policy. She believed it would be wrong to obscure the baptism she had already received. How could she be the recipient of an additional baptism when the Scriptures teach but one baptism? Why was her new church demanding a second baptism? Were they declaring her first baptism invalid? No one sat down with her to investigate the validity of her first baptism, and no one wanted to acknowledge any beauty or benefits from her first baptism. Debbie felt condemned and second-class. She became confused. Whose baptism was right and whose was wrong? One thing was certain: she didn't like the subject of baptism anymore. Its beauty and benefit seemed to fade and no one seemed to care as long as she conformed to the ritual as others understood it. Is it lawful to glorify man or God with the doctrine and practice of baptism? Is it lawful to strengthen and encourage the saints or to weaken, confuse, and discourage them with baptism?

Many marriages, families, churches, and individuals have parted company over the issue of baptism. That's not right and we know it. As members of the body of Christ, we are not to be divided.

We are called to "walk in a manner worthy of the calling with which you have been called, with all humility and gentleness, with patience, showing tolerance for one another in love, being diligent to preserve the unity of the Spirit in the bond of peace" (Eph. 4:1-3). Since there is but "one Lord, one faith, one baptism" (Eph. 4:5), some of us are wrong on its interpretation (some a little wrong and some a lot). Nevertheless, that is no reason to get controversial and divisive with one another. Let us be subdued by the Word of God. The wrangling over opinions is endless and fruitless, not to mention harmful to Christian fellowship. We are called upon to destroy those speculations which are contrary to the knowledge of God and take every thought captive to the obedience of Christ (2 Cor. 10:5). We must open our minds along with our Bibles and be conformed to God's truth. No one can claim to be open-minded who is afraid to evaluate his beliefs and practices with God's Word (2 Tim. 2:15). Can we prove through biblical references and arguments what we believe about baptism, and can we show how such faith is consistent with all the related passages of Scripture? If not, then let us work on getting beyond our opinions, and even though they may be right, let us labor until they are substantiated by a consistent interpretation of the whole counsel of God.

I challenged a Southern Baptist pastor to weekly dialogue on baptism until we became like-minded on the subject (2 Cor. 13:11) and he accepted. He was convinced that repentance and faith in Christ should always precede water baptism and that baptism should only be administered to believers and not their children (until their children repented of sin and embraced Christ by faith). He believed that immersion was the only proper mode for such baptism. I grew up in Baptist and Methodist churches, but I grew more and more accepting of a Reformed and Presbyterian perspective. Who was right? Those were interesting and sanctifying meetings. We both grew in appreciation for the Scripture's sufficiency to answer all our doubts, fears, and arguments of preference. God led us to peace and love and a unity of doctrine that has been ordained for all of those in Christ Jesus (John 17:17-23). How good it is to dwell together with brothers in unity!

It is not enough to say we believe something. We must believe what we believe because it is based on the factual, inerrant truth of the Bible. The Christian faith is not a "leap in the dark." We believe what we believe because of God's divine disclosure through the written Word of God. God wants us to be both sanctified and unified in his truth (John 17:17-23). Unsanctified relationships and discord break out in the body of Christ when we stray from our responsibility to study Scripture and handle it accurately in a manner leading to purity and unity. Sadly, not enough Christians have attempted this in the area of church sacraments. My desire in this book is to unfold the beauty and benefits of baptism. I am not on a mission to prove anybody wrong or to condemn anyone for their contrary views. As a matter of fact, I would have us begin with a study on how to love the people who differ with us on issues like baptism.

Practically speaking, we must hear our brothers and sisters out. If they have a different view on baptism, then we must practice submission to one another out of reverence for Christ (Eph. 5:21). We can have all the knowledge in the world and even the correct views on baptism, but without love for our brethren we are not doing church right and our value is zero—nothing (1 Cor. 13:2). Because of our commitment to love God with all our being and our neighbor as ourselves (Matt. 22:36-40), we must resolve our differences and agree to work together until we are of one mind on the matter of baptism. We are not free to shun, condemn, or demean one another. We must strive for like-mindedness. We must not remain silent but speak to one another in truth and love until we reach the unity of the Spirit in the bond of peace.

Christ alone is King and head of the church (Eph. 1:22), and his authority reigns supreme (Col. 1:18). His word alone is truth (John 17:17). He directs how we are to worship him (Exod. 20:4-6). Furthermore, the Lord forbids us from adding to or taking away from his commands (Deut. 4:2; 12:32; Prov. 30:6; Rev. 2:18-19). What he says about baptism in his Word settles the issue—whether or not we choose to believe it or enjoy it. This must be our starting conviction.

Therefore, as we approach a study of baptism, I invite you to come armed with the helmet of salvation and the sword of the Spirit, which is the Word of God, and I will do the same (Eph. 6:17). Let us examine the Scriptures to see if what we hear on this subject is true (Acts 17:11). Let us lay aside our sentimental attachment to opinions, superstitions, and traditions that have no biblical basis. Let the outcome of our views on baptism hang only upon the teaching of the Bible and nothing more. If I am wrong, then use God's written revelation to refute me so we may be one in the truth. Let us together ask God for wisdom that we might be sanctified by his grace and for his glory.

Perhaps it is worth mentioning that in this book on baptism you will find a few things you don't frequently find in books of this sort. First is a lay-friendly and pastoral style, with many Scripture references printed within the text for easy checking. There is a lengthy section on the specific benefits and blessings of infant baptism (seven in all) that will deeply satisfy parents who have been asking, "Is it really worth it?" The book begins with a chapter on love, since few of us want or feel any need to get involved in another divisive and argumentative church controversy. There are over one hundred Bible references to sprinkling or pouring listed right from the Bible. To my knowledge, such a list has never been presented in a baptism book, thus leaving many students of the subject with no true sense of the "first hearers' first century context." One of the foundational principles of accurate Bible interpretation is ascertaining how and why the first audience understood the message. There is also a brief exposition on Jesus' comments regarding his baptism that I have yet to see included in a book on baptism. And what could be more important than Jesus telling us firsthand how he was baptized and what it means? The issue of how we are to improve our baptism is only addressed with confidence after we determine whether or not our baptism is valid. In the appendix, there is a sample infant baptism service for those who are ready to consider the practice of covenantal baptism using appropriate Scripture, prayer, vows, and praise. These things which are not usually found in baptism books are accompanied by all of the things you might expect: explanations on the meaning and mode of baptism, the origin and symbolism of baptism, and arguments for and against immersion and sprinkling.

May this study bring all of my readers much delight through growth in the truth and heart of God. May you gain tools and truth to encourage and train your children and all the family of God. May you benefit greatly from the work of his Spirit and may you gain such confidence in this subject that it increases your joy in worship and unity in fellowship with your brothers and sisters in Christ.

Chapter 1

A Beautiful and Beneficial Tool

A COUPLE CAME to me for premarital counseling. She was a member at a conservative evangelical Presbyterian church. He was a Southern Baptist preacher. They were engaged to be married, and I was chosen to assist them in their preparations and wedding ceremony. Among other things, we discussed potential areas of conflict in their future marriage, not the least of which would be the baptism of their children.

For him, to baptize his children as infants just might require him to renounce his standing as a Southern Baptist preacher, something he did not intend to do. For her to neglect having her children baptized as infants would be sinful—a covenantal break with God, not to mention an act of difficult submission to her husband. Just bringing up the inevitable serious conflict down the road caused much inward grief for both of them. We determined to study the subject of infant baptism with the commitment to love one another regardless of whether or not our prior conclusions on the subject changed. My goal as a counselor was not primarily for this couple to reach the same view on baptism (like-mindedness can be achieved, but I wasn't as optimistic in those days). My goal for him was that he demonstrate his willingness to lay down his life for her and love her as Christ loved the church, respecting her value as a co-heir with Christ and her wisdom learned at the feet of Christ. My goal for her was that she respect her husband's convictions about baptism so highly that she could gladly submit to his leadership and live as one.

The preacher grew to live with his wife in an understanding way and to appreciate her wisdom, even in deep theological matters. The wife learned to respect her husband and to submit to his loving authority. They began with a strong disagreement over their baptism views, but they live today in the bonds of love and peace as a result of a careful study of God's Word and a willing submission to it. For them, baptism became a beautiful tool for developing deeper love for God and one another.

Jesus prayed for his church, that she would be unified in truth (John 17:13-23). He has given to us divine revelation, his Word, so that we would not find our direction from the world but from our Creator and God (17:14). He pleads with the Father to sanctify us in this word which is the truth of God (17:17-19). For all who believe in his Word as the only infallible rule of faith and practice, Jesus prayed that we would be unified in it. Our unity is in his truth. If we are not unified, then we have departed from his truth. The only way we can be "perfected in unity" (17:23) is for us to be perfected in our understanding and application of God's truth.

I have often been asked, "How can there be only one Bible and one accurate interpretation of that Bible, and yet so many seemingly godly individuals reach different conclusions about what the Bible says?" The answer to this question is that when we reach different conclusions, some of us are wrong and others are right. Of course, there is also the possibility that we are both wrong. The very fact that Jesus prayed that we would be sanctified in the truth is an acknowledgment that we are prone to stray from the truth when we cease to yield to the sanctifying work of the Holy Spirit. Consequently, many divisions, even into various denominations, have occurred within the true church and body of the Lord Jesus Christ. Though the divisions obscure the visible unity of the body of Christ, they do not destroy it. Such divisions would only destroy the visible unity of the body of Christ if we were to allow them to become impregnable barriers that forbid fellowship and dialogue with those who are our brothers and sisters in God's covenant of grace. We must diligently work for the unity Christ intended us to enjoy. We must learn to love Christians with whom we differ and conform our differences to Scripture until we are one in the truth.

Different Views on Baptism				
	Mode or Method	Who is Baptized	Meaning of Baptism	Rationale
1st View: Baptist, Pentecostals, Charismatics, Independents, Others	Immersion	1. Adult Believers 2. Baby Dedications (not baptisms)	A memorial sign of salvation ("death to sin and new life in Christ")	1. Follow Jesus in immersion 2. Rom. 6:4-6
2nd View: Church of Christ	Immersion	Adult Believers	Salvation	1 Pet. 3:21, "Baptism saves you"
3rd View: Roman Catholic	Sprinkling	1. Infants 2. Adult Converts to the Roman Catholic Faith	1. It removes Adam's sinful nature in you 2. It removes actual sin	1. The view of the church that partial forgiveness can be granted 2. Same as above
4th View: Methodists, Episcopalians, Lutherans, Others	Sprinkling	1. Infants 2. Adult Converts	1. A dedication to the Lord 2. A profession of faith in Christ	1. 1 Sam. 1:27-28 2. Acts 2:38-39
5th View: Reformed Independents, Reformed Presbyterians, Others	Sprinkling	1. Infants of parents who profess faith in Christ 2. Adults who profess faith in Christ	1. Sign and seal of God's Covenant union 2. Sign and seal of God's covenant union	1. Gen. 17:7, 11; Rom. 4:11; Acts 2:39 2. Acts 2:38, 39; Matt. 28:19, 20

Since the right administration of the sacraments is a mark of a true church worthy of our support, trivializing this doctrinal matter will not be a good strategy for peace or unity. At the same time, however, we must learn how not to break fellowship over it. Consider the chart above—a sign of how the church has been divided and broken over baptism. For each different view of baptism, consider what is fairly said and what is unfair, what is accurate and inaccurate. Rarely could this chart be presented to a group of believers where someone would not want to adjust something more in line with their understanding or experience. It is difficult getting our hands around all our differences since many local churches teach many different things. But after seeing the perceived differences we have over this issue, we can understand why we need to be committed to love each other first. Unity can be restored, but not without love.

In an attempt to strengthen the bonds of love and unity in Christ, as opposed to causing further divisions within the body, let me suggest guidelines we should employ when we find ourselves united to Christians with different baptism views. Obviously, the principles I suggest may be easily applied to other issues beyond baptism.

Destroy Pride

First, we must acknowledge and renounce our own personal pride and presumption. In Ephesians 4:1-2, God reveals that the only way we are going to be able to bear with one another in love is through humility, gentleness, patience, and showing tolerance for one another in love. The term *humility* means to be lowly minded. It means not to exalt ourselves. It is an acknowledgment that we are not the most important people on the planet. According to the second chapter of Ephesians, we are dead in our trespasses and sins except by the grace and mercy of God. God is in charge, not us. Our pride, then, is utter foolishness and presumption. If we let it run unchecked, it breeds contempt for others. It is impossible that we will be in agreement with others until we first learn to rid ourselves of pride and presumption. Being humble, gentle, and patient is not so much a determination to be nice as it is a conviction that God has chosen us to be who we are and has taught us what we know. When we think our correct views on baptism are the result of our own keen intellect and human cleverness, we tend to relegate those with different views to a realm of stupidity or laziness. This is not good for unity.

Consider 1 Corinthians 4:7: "For who regards you as superior? What do you have that you did not receive? And if you did receive it, why do you boast as if you had not received it?" The apostle Paul makes it clear that it is foolish for us to boast as though we are above other men. What we have, we have been given by God. Therefore, we are to honor God for it rather than ourselves. Those of us who know ourselves best will esteem ourselves least. If God has given us the truth on the issue of baptism, it was not so we could boast about it and hold others in contempt for their ignorance. God has given us what we have so that we will honor him and love one another.

When we truly love other people, we will not brag or be arrogant about what we know or have accomplished (1 Cor. 13:4). If we cannot discuss the matter of baptism without boasting, it would be better for us to never discuss it at all. Our goal in presenting God's Word to others is to draw them to God, to win them to him, rather than to embitter them through our arrogance, contempt, or spite. When speaking to those for whom Christ has died, let us be careful to always edify.

> Let no unwholesome word proceed from your mouth, but only such a word as is good for edification according to the need of the moment, so that it will give grace to those who hear. Do not grieve the Holy Spirit of God, by whom you were sealed for the day of redemption. Let all bitterness and wrath and anger and clamor and slander be put away from you, along with all malice. Be kind to one another, tender-hearted, forgiving each other, just as God in Christ also has forgiven you.
>
> —Eph. 4:29-32

When we begin our day with God and our discussions with others as debtors to grace, then we are far more likely to acknowledge our fallibility and demonstrate that we are far more interested in the discovery of God's truth than we are in exalting our knowledge or winning an argument. We must invite and welcome correction from error and the beauty of being conformed more to Christ's image through understanding more fully the benefits of his revelation. What can we learn from those who differ from us on baptism? We agree there is much room for further sanctification, so let us denounce our pride and open ourselves up to correction in Christ.

Develop Perspective

Second, we must distinguish between believers and unbelievers and be sensitive to their different needs. When dealing with people who differ from us on doctrinal issues such as baptism, we must not only avoid the temptation of developing an overly judgmental spirit, but we must nevertheless discern to the best of our ability whether or not the one with whom we differ is a believer or unbeliever in Christ. Christians and non-Christians do not have the same needs. Christians need to grow in maturity, turning from their ignorance and shallowness towards depth and purity of doctrine. Non-Christians need Jesus Christ as their Lord and Savior, plain and simple. They don't need to get bogged down in the details of the church and its sacraments until they have surrendered through faith and repentance to the head of the church who is Jesus Christ.

> Conduct yourselves with wisdom toward outsiders, making the most of the opportunity. Let your speech always be with grace, as though seasoned with salt, so that you will know how you should respond to each person.
>
> —Col. 4:5-6

Conducting ourselves with wisdom requires us to know who is in the church and who is not. When we speak with those outside the church, it is foolish to bicker with the details of church doctrine. Their need is not to quarrel but to see the sufficiency of Jesus Christ for all things.

Suppose a non-Christian wants to talk about the differences between our view of baptism and the view of baptism he was taught. What should we do then? We need to quickly show him he will not understand the implications of baptism until he understands and embraces the author of that sacrament, Jesus Christ. The non-Christian cannot accept the things of the Spirit of God until he has the Spirit of God within.

> For to us God revealed them through the Spirit; for the Spirit searches all things, even the depths of God. For who among men knows the thoughts of a man except the spirit of the man which is in him? Even so the thoughts of God no one knows except the Spirit of God. Now we have received, not the spirit of the world, but the Spirit who is from God, so that we may know the things freely given to us by God, which things we also speak, not in words taught by human wisdom, but in those taught by the Spirit, combining spiritual thoughts with spiritual words. But a natural man does not accept the things of the Spirit of God, for they are foolishness to him; and he cannot understand them, because they are spiritually appraised.
>
> —1 Cor. 2:10-14

Whenever we speak with non-Christians, we should not argue over doctrinal details, but rather gently teach the beauty and glory of Christ. That way, God might work through us and grant them repentance and the understanding to embrace the whole truth of God's Word and escape the snare of the Devil (2 Tim. 2:24-26). We need to live evangelistically so people will ask us about the hope within us so that we may respond to them with gentleness and reverence, leading them to Christ (1 Pet. 3:15).

When we differ with non-Christians, we need to respond to them with compassionate evangelism. Never should we allow baptism or any of its ramifications to be used to skirt the issue of a rebellious heart. Let us deal with people according to their most important need. If it is for salvation, then let us deal with them concerning Christ. If it is for maturity in Christ, then let us join in fellowship around the doctrines of Christ. Christians and non-Christians will not become like-minded over discussions of the glory and love of God in baptism until the non-Christian is converted to Christ. Let us develop a perspective enabling us to speak to Christians and non-Christians alike with love.

Demonstrate Patience

Third, we must maintain the unity of the Spirit by showing tolerance with humility, gentleness, and patience. Ephesians 4:1-6 speaks to the issue of unity in the church.

> Walk in a manner worthy of the calling with which you have been called, with all humility and gentleness, with patience, showing tolerance for one another in love, being diligent to preserve the unity of the Spirit in the bond of peace. There is one body and one Spirit, just as also you were called in one hope of your calling; one Lord, one faith, one baptism, one God and Father of all who is over all and through all and in all.

Christians are to make every effort to maintain unity. We are not to seek division over doctrinal concerns. We are to maintain or preserve unity—in other words, we are to guard our unity just as we would guard a prisoner behind bars. We need to bring our unity under protective custody.

What is the unity we are called to maintain? God tells us that as the church we are of "one body and one Spirit just as also you were called in one hope of your calling, one Lord, one faith, one baptism, one God and Father of all who is over all and through all and in all." The unity, then, is based on God and what he has done. We are not to quarrel over what kind of God he is, or what manner of baptism he has given us. Rather, we are to recognize first and foremost that he has drawn us to himself as one unified people, and we must make every effort to remain that way.

Consider how the subject of baptism is used in the apostle Paul's letter to the Galatians:

> For all of you who were baptized into Christ have clothed yourselves with Christ. There is neither Jew nor Greek, there is neither slave nor free man, there is neither male nor female; for you are all one in Christ Jesus (3:27-28).

Paul uses the argument of our unity in baptism to point us to Christ, not to division. Notice that when he thinks of baptism ("all of you who were baptized"), he thinks of our unity ("you are all one"). Isn't that interesting? Baptism does not remind God (and it should not remind us) that there are different baptisms for different people. There is only one baptism for everyone who is united to Christ. Baptism was designed as a beautiful tool and sign of unity. There are not different baptisms for those of different races, for males or for females, for children or for adults. There is but one baptism. The reason there is but one baptism is because there is only one covenant between God and his people. It consecrates us to him as our one Lord and Redeemer. If we allow baptism to divide us, then we obscure one of the very significant things baptism was given to teach us, and that is our one covenantal union with our God and his people. If we allow baptism to divide us, then we are hardly "being diligent to preserve the unity of the Spirit in the bond of peace" (Eph. 4:3).

When we divide ourselves, we are in some sense estranged from God. This is not to say that we must pursue peace at all cost. There is no peace which is commendable by Scripture unless it joins us and keeps us together under one God. When we seek union with people, we must always have as our primary goal union with God. We are not truly at peace if we find unity with a person who separates us from intimacy with God. Proper unity binds us together as brothers and sisters *in Christ*, walking together in concord and brotherly love. God is neither separated nor divided in and of himself. Since we are in God and God is in us, there should be no division among us, either. After all, there is but "one

God and Father of all who is over all and through all and in all" (Eph. 4:6). A right understanding of baptism should lead us closer to God and to one another. Therefore, in dealing with the issue of baptism, we must do so in a manner maintaining unity of Spirit in the bond of peace.

Do Preparation

Fourth, we must study to show ourselves approved unto God. Paul told us to "be diligent to present yourself approved to God as a workman who does not need to be ashamed, accurately handling the word of truth" (2 Tim. 2:15). When we don't agree with someone else on a particular matter, like the subject of baptism, it is much easier to assume we are right than it is to prove we are right. Similarly, it is easier to assume correct teaching from someone (like our childhood pastor or parents) than it is to check it out and to verify its faithfulness to the Word of God, as we are encouraged to do in Acts 17:11. The Scriptures warn us that it is not easy to hold to sound doctrine. (2 Tim. 4:3-5). The exhortation "to endure sound doctrine" requires us to stick with it even when it is difficult. But many would rather people simply tell them something that sounds good and something they like, rather than tell them something they might need to check out before following.

The tendency of many is to follow what makes sense as opposed to what might not make sense and yet be more consistent with the whole counsel of God. We are commanded in such cases to "be sober in all things" and to "endure hardship" (4:5). In other words, we are commanded "to keep our head," to "maintain our sanity," and to not follow our desires but endure the hardship and difficulties that come with faithfully clinging to God's Word and work.

A good friend named Bill came to me one day asking about God's love for the world, as recorded in John 3:16 ("For God so loved the world, that He gave His only begotten Son, that whoever believes in Him shall not perish, but have eternal life"). I had recently referred to God's love for the world as not necessarily including everyone, since the Scripture plainly says God hated Esau (Mal. 1:3; Rom. 9:13). Bill then wanted to know what to do with John 3:16. My response was that we were forced into more in-depth study, not into disagreement. It is so much easier to simply write people off and to disagree with them than to strive for like-mindedness with them through Bible research.

We quickly found that there were 190 references to *world* in the New American Standard translation. When we began looking at them all, we discovered the word *world* had a world of meanings. Without careful study, we could easily be confused by the term. For example, in John 3:16, God is said to love the world, and yet in 1 John 2:15 we are commanded, "Do not love the world nor the things in the world. If anyone loves the world, the love of the Father is not in him." The texts make sense when we agree that *world* has more than one meaning. In each case, we must find a sure clue to the meaning of the word within its immediate context. It might be referring to the Roman world or empire (Luke 2:1, Acts 11:28); humanity's material dwelling place, the globe (Ps. 33:8); the whole universe (Ps. 90:2); the values of unbelievers (James 1:27, 1 John 2:15); material possessions (Matt. 16:26); depraved human thinking (1 Cor. 3:19); the unrepentant, non-elect people (John 14:17, 19; 17:9); the redeemed, elect people of God (John 1:29; 3:16, 17; 4:42; 8:12); a kingdom contrary to the kingdom of Christ (John 18:36, 37); humankind in general (Rom. 5:12, 13); or something else (this list is not exhaustive).

Bill and I concluded our study in one mind that John 3:16 might more likely be referring to a love from God which included all of the geography he had created and every ethnic group in those places. This left room for the anger and wrath of God without diminishing his passion to take the good news of his kingdom to all who would believe. My like-mindedness with Bill did not grow as long as one of us was content with a view of *world* that was "half-baked" rather than "full-orbed."

In Paul's second letter to Timothy, we are commanded to "be diligent to present yourself approved to God as a workman who does not need to be ashamed, accurately handling the word of truth" (2:15). When it comes to the issue of baptism, will we be able to stand before God unashamed at the way we have studied the matter? Are we like the good Berean Christians who have studied everything we have been taught regarding baptism to see whether or not it is consistent with everything God has revealed in the scriptures (Acts 17:11)? For example, suppose someone teaches us that every time they find baptism in the New Testament, it follows repentance. Therefore, they make the assertion that personal faith and repentance is a prerequisite to every baptism. Will we be so swayed by this assertion that we refuse to entertain the possibility of children being baptized prior to faith and repentance? In the Old Testament, proof of keeping the covenant was never a prerequisite to receiving the sign of the covenant, namely circumcision. Children were circumcised at eight days old, prior to any acts of covenantal faithfulness (Gen. 17:12). There are a multitude of references to being circumcised prior to being held responsible for embracing all the obligations of God's covenant with man. Circumcision came first. Faith and repentance followed. If circumcision was replaced by baptism, then does the order of applying the sacrament prior to faith and repentance remain or is there some reason for an adjustment? To answer this question, one must study the Scriptures to see whether or not there is continuity between the Old and New Testaments, whether baptism does indeed replace circumcision, and whether or not the New Testament changes the previous practice of covenant keeping.

There are passages of Scripture that need to be studied, like the story of Simon in Acts 8:13-24. If Simon genuinely believed in Christ, it was *after* being baptized as an adult. Simon may never have had saving faith and genuine repentance, and it would be wrong for us to assume this since we are never shown or told of his genuine faith in Christ. But he did have adult baptism.

There is also the passage regarding Isaac, who was circumcised (i.e. Old Testament baptism) as an infant prior to being saved: "Then Abraham circumcised his son Isaac when he was eight days old, as God had commanded him" (Gen. 21:4). Indeed, all of Israel under Moses was baptized (adults and children), even though most of them were not saved and pleasing to God (1 Cor. 10:2-5). Baptisms prior to conversion propose a problem for many of us. The whole matter demands study if we are to reach the unity God has designed for our joy and his glory.

Suppose someone has a question on the proper mode for baptism. There is no explicit command in the Bible anywhere to immerse anyone, nor is there any explicit command for infant baptism. Some have assumed that immersion is the proper way to interpret the term *baptism*, even though there are over two hundred references in Scripture to sprinkling and pouring, with hardly any specific references to immersing. Will we assume a way of baptizing that God nowhere explicitly commands, or will we study (even if it requires research on more than two hundred references) to find what he clearly directs through his own infallible revelation to us? Will we study to see whether or not we have an "every tribe, tongue, and nation" view of baptism? Does God demand a way of baptizing his disciples in every ethnic group (Matt. 28:18-20) which would be impossible to carry out? Missionaries have told me stories of baptizing in places where it was so cold their spit froze before it reached the ground. In other places there was very little water that could be found. The church is growing among those on sick beds, in icy climates, desert regions, and in other places where God's saints must postpone baptism if they seek immersion. How does God's word (not our inventions) address such things?

Christ chastises the religious leaders of his day for not reading and knowing the Hebrew Scriptures thoroughly. Over and over again, Jesus asked them whether or not they had read the Scriptures ("Have you not read...." Matt. 12:3, 5; 19:4; 21:16, 42; 22:31). Obviously, they would have been happy to give witness to anyone prior to Christ's remarks that they had read the Scriptures and were knowledgeable in them. Nevertheless, they came up short before Christ for not knowing the Scriptures rightly. They had allowed themselves to make assumptions concerning God's Word without truly studying it.

We should not simply assume we know and understand everything there is to know on the subject of baptism. Instead, we need to study it in such detail that we can prove our convictions with love for each other so we can stand before God without shame.

Deliver Prodding

A fifth guideline to employ when we find ourselves around brothers and sisters in Christ who have different baptism views is to admonish them for growth and edification. If we have conflicting views regarding the meaning, mode, recipients, or benefits of baptism, then obviously, one of us is wrong. Quite possibly, both of us are wrong. The Word of God is flawless, but we are human and prone to error. After we have evaluated our own hearts and become convinced that we are not arrogantly assuming our view is right, and after we have thoroughly studied every portion of God's Word on the matter to firm up our convictions in a consistent manner, then we have the obligation to admonish other members of the body of Christ with humility, gentleness, and love.

The word *admonish* can mean to advise, warn, teach, spur on, and to remind someone again. There are times when we need to hear God's Word more than once, sometimes many times, before we truly understand it and its implications. Thus, we need the loving admonitions of those spiritually fit to provide them (Rom. 15:14-15). The apostle Paul knew that there were many good people in the church at Rome who were able to teach and prod their brothers along in the Scriptures. Nevertheless, they needed to be reminded more boldly by him, especially since God had given him special grace to strongly teach the Word of God. In the same way, if we have been granted the grace to understand God's covenant with his creation and the sign of that covenant, which is a matter so deep and extensive and yet so rich and wonderful that we cannot keep it to ourselves, we are required by God to admonish those who have yet to get it.

Biblical unity obligates us to admonish one another (Eph. 4:3, 12-16). If we are diligent to preserve the unity of the Spirit, then we must not let the body of Christ split and divide over doctrinal issues like baptism. We must listen to those who are pastors and teachers to be equipped so that we can all attain to the unity of the faith (4:13). We are not to be tossed to and fro by every wind of doctrine, but must speak the truth to one another in love, so that we grow through that which every joint supplies (4:14-16). One of the reasons there is such lack of understanding on the subject of baptism is because many of the people who have known the truth have not taken up the responsibility to explain it to others.

I have often found that my dear brothers and sisters in Christ who are convinced that baptism is to be performed by immersion are those I know who are most passionate about global missions. Yet some are willing to neglect their own family worship times, doctrinal instruction of their children, and Sabbath observance to pursue their passion for missions. On the other hand, those saints who are consistent in family devotional times and the raising of their children for Christ often lean heavily towards infant baptism and its covenant implications, yet some of them can neglect global missions. Don't both groups need to lovingly admonish the other? It is sad that we live during a time where many children are raised up to have their own way. Infant baptism seems to be an absurdity because we have neglected to teach the beauty and benefits of rearing children who are not their own masters. They are under the sovereign ownership of God and their parents are obligated to raise them as such. They are to be marked out and distinguished in society as God's holy ones, sanctified through the biblical duties of godly parents (Eph. 6:1-4; 1 Cor. 7:14).

We need to understand that biblical admonition is a loving work, and those who do it should be esteemed very highly (1 Thess. 5:12-15). We are to hold the people who remind us of the truth of God's Word in the highest regard. Their instruction keeps us from being undisciplined and unruly in our behavior, and it strengthens us when we are weak and enables us to live at peace with one another. Let us then not only be open to admonishing one another, since that is our divine obligation, but also be open to receiving admonishment, since it is God's means for our edification.

There is a need in the heat of admonition to listen to one another for the general more than for the precise. Often the precise articulation of a matter comes through the fire of admonition, so let us be quick to get the benefit of admonition even if the precise language used is not entirely accurate. For example, I am guilty of exaggeration at times. I say words like *never* and *always* when I mean *rarely* and *frequently*. I have said, "Baptism *never* means immersion," when what I really mean is that baptism *rarely* means immersion. The fact that it *can* mean immersion, but does not always mean this, means we have work to do, to see when and how often God uses it this way. Someone may say, "Baptism *always* follows repentance," when what they really mean is that it *frequently* follows repentance. During admonition, if you quibble over my words or I quibble over yours, we may miss the truth and the benefits of growing closer together. Admonition done and received rightly is a beautiful thing that unites the body of Christ. Let us not miss this blessing of love. Denominational barriers have greatly inhibited this loving admonition and all believers need to be working to remedy this situation.

Definitely Pray

Do the difficulties with baptism sometimes make us grieve and pray? What is the net result when someone disagrees with us on baptism? If it merely wounds our ego or crushes our pride, then let us thank God—since that usually needs to take place. We are probably the ones who need admonition to change our position and bring it into conformity with God's teaching. But if the result of a disagreement between us and someone else leads to their suffering and harm, we should not go our own way rejoicing that we have a handle on the truth and they do not. Rather, we should grieve when our brethren are missing the benefits of God's covenant grace, and we should pray that they soon experience them.

The apostle Paul warned the church of Ephesus that people would seek to feed them deadly poison and teach them perverse things to draw them away from the truth:

> Keep watch over yourselves and all the flock of which the Holy Spirit has made you overseers. Be shepherds of the church of God, which he bought with his own blood. I know that after I leave,

> savage wolves will come in among you and will not spare the flock. Even from your own number men will arise and distort the truth in order to draw away disciples after them. So be on your guard! Remember that for three years I never stopped warning each of you night and day with tears. Now I commit you to God and to the word of his grace, which can build you up and give you an inheritance among all those who are sanctified.
>
> —Acts 20:28-32

Consequently, there was a need for elders (overseers) in the church to guard the flock from inaccurate doctrine. Paul tells us that during the three years he was in Ephesus he did not cease to admonish the believers "with tears" and commit them to God, presumably through prayer. Here we have the example of Paul responding to Christians who have a tendency to believe wrong things, so much so that he wept because he knew what suffering erroneous teaching can cause. His grief leads him beyond admonition to pray for the body of Christ to be sanctified and built up through the Word of God.

When people misunderstand God's revelation on baptism, they typically obscure God's wonderful covenantal grace to promote human responsiveness. They completely miss the significance of Christ's being the Anointed One, the sinless Savior, the Messiah through his baptism in the third chapter of the gospel of Matthew. Further, they miss the radical breach with sin given the believer as described in Romans chapter six through our union with Christ's death, burial, and resurrection. They also miss the connection between the ritual mode of baptism and the real spiritual baptism through the work of the Holy Spirit coming down upon us. They seek to improve their baptisms through outward rebaptisms, rather than through inward transformation. They miss the glorious continuity of the covenant in the Old Testament with the covenant in the New Testament. They miss many rich, rewarding, and eternally significant benefits for their children and their family life; they miss all of this and more. I think this is sad. I don't get angry with those who have yet to understand baptism. I hurt for them and I commend them to God through prayer.

God exhorts us to pray for one another so we can all lead a tranquil and quiet life in all godliness and holiness (1 Tim. 2:1-8). The Lord wants us to pray for each other, and especially for those who are in authority over us. When they teach us things or lead us in ways that upset us, instead of becoming angry and being divisive, God wants us to lift up holy hands and pray. He wants us to lead people to a position of unity with our God and peaceful fellowship with one another. As much as it is possible, we must not respond to those who differ with us by getting mad at them and leaving them, but rather by grieving and praying for them.

Devise Praise

Seventh, rejoice and pray. It might seem contradictory at first that we should grieve and pray, and then rejoice and pray over the same issue. How is it that we can have strong doctrinal disagreement and misinterpretation between us and another brother in Christ and then expect to rejoice? Just as we should grieve because one of us in the disagreement is wrong, we can also rejoice because there is the strong possibility that the other party in the disagreement is right. Love rejoices with the truth (1 Cor. 13:6). Regardless of who possesses the truth first, we should rejoice if it is possessed by the body of Christ.

Since God "gave himself for us to redeem us from all wickedness and to purify for himself a people that are his very own, eager to do what is good" (Titus 2:14), every disagreement between us and another believer is an opportunity for our growth in sanctification. God has given us brothers and sisters in Christ who can help us. We need them. Every member of the body of Christ has been given gifts by God for the common good (1 Cor. 12:7). Let us pray that just as iron sharpens iron, we would sharpen one another (Prov. 27:17). Let us pray through an abundance of godly counselors God would give us wisdom (Prov. 11:14; 15:22; 24:6). We must also pray constantly that God would reveal to us what is truly in our hearts and sanctify us if we have any wicked things within (Ps. 139:23).

Imagine what life would be like if, every time we found ourselves in disagreement with other Christians, we first dealt with all the sin that was within our own hearts? If we did that, we could embrace all fellow Christians as our dearest brothers and sisters in Christ. We would be able to preserve the unity of the Spirit and set ourselves upon a disciplined course of studying God's Word to determine the reason for our differences. We would admonish one another with the fruit of our Bible study and always pray for one another to be more and more like Jesus. It would be a wonderful thing, dealing with our own sin like that. God hates those who spread strife among their brothers (Prov. 6:16, 19), but his blessings abound when we pursue peace and unity, loving one another through our differences.

We clearly have an obligation to the truth, but we must always speak that truth in love. Baptism needs to be used again as a tool of love and unity to bring God's people together in the worship and joy of our Lord. As we study this subject, let us "walk in a manner worthy of the calling with which we have been called, with all humility and gentleness, with patience, showing tolerance for one another in love, being diligent to preserve the unity of the Spirit in the bond of peace. There is one body and one Spirit, just as also you were called in one hope of your calling; one Lord, one faith, *one baptism*, one God and Father of all who is over all and through all and in all" (Eph. 4:1-6, emphasis added). "Finally, brethren, rejoice, be made complete, be comforted, be like-minded, live in peace; and the God of love and peace will be with you. Greet one another with a holy kiss. All the saints greet you. The grace of the Lord Jesus Christ, and the love of God, and the fellowship of the Holy Spirit, be with you all" (2 Cor. 13:11-14).

Discussion and Study Questions

1. How important is it to God that his children dwell together in unity and be like-minded regarding doctrine? Consider John 17:13-23, Acts 1:14; 2:46, Romans 12:16; 15:5, 1 Corinthians 1:10, and Philippians 1:27. What kinds of things must we do to achieve greater like-mindedness?

2. How can doctrinal disagreements become tools in the hand of God for our growth in grace and love?
3. John Calvin has been quoted as saying no theologian is ever more than eighty percent right. If we knew where our twenty percent of error was, wouldn't we correct it? How valuable then is it to listen to and evaluate what is said by those who disagree with us? What place should love have in this dialogue, and how do we achieve it?
4. What do you like and dislike about the information contained in the chart on "Different Views on Baptism"? Why?
5. What issues besides baptism tend to divide genuine believers of Christ? What can be done to bring unity on these issues?
6. Do you agree or disagree with this statement? "If we cannot discuss the matter of baptism without boasting, it would be better for us to never discuss the matter at all."
7. What are the difficulties associated with maintaining an eternal perspective on people, always seeking to discern whether they are headed to heaven or hell? How can these difficulties be overcome?
8. In what ways have you seen baptism used to divide true believers? Is the work of Satan in your perspective? In what ways have you seen baptism unite true believers? How can baptism be better used as a sign and tool of Christian unity?
9. What personal examples can you give of the truth of this statement, "It is much easier to assume we are right than it is to prove we are right. Similarly, it is easier to assume correct teaching from someone than it is to check it out and to verify its faithfulness to the Word of God."
10. How is the concept of prodding one another along in the Scriptures to occur if we are not gifted as pastors or teachers? How often? In what context?

11. What have denominational barriers done to inhibit loving and biblical brotherly admonition? What can we do to remedy this situation?
12. We might think of various ways to respond when other people fail to appreciate our discussions/admonitions on baptism. What would be our best response to them?

Chapter 2

The Beautiful and Beneficial Message of Baptism

IF BAPTISM ALWAYS means immersion, then it would be important to know that before we begin a study on how to do it or on how to gain benefit from it. Knowing what a word means, or how an author uses a word, is crucial to our understanding of his thoughts and intentions. For example, I was changing my son's diaper when my friend said, "He baptized you!" I replied, "Yep, he sure did, and next time I will let you change his diapers." What did my friend mean by *baptized* in this context? While washing an automobile, I was threatened by another friend who was holding a bucket of water. "Hurry up, or I will baptize you," he warned. What did this friend mean by the word *baptize*? One more example: While fishing with two seminary buddies, one stood up in the end of the boat to untangle his line from a low hanging tree limb. The other protested, "Don't stand up or we may all be baptized!" What did he mean?

The word *baptism* may be used in many different ways, and it can mean different things. It can refer to sprinkling, pouring, or immersion, as illustrated from the above examples. The question before us is what does God mean by the word and sacrament of baptism? The fact that God could use the term in different ways requires us to avoid reaching conclusions about the Bible's use of the term prior to a thorough investigation of the context in which it is used.

I was attending a Bible conference where the wonderful preaching of God's Word went forth with power and conviction from a very famous Baptist preacher. During the question and answer period of the conference, someone asked the speaker a question concerning his view of baptism. He explained he believed in total immersion. Since he seemed to wholeheartedly embrace the doctrines of God's covenant love and grace, why did he not also embrace baptism as a covenant sign for his children? His answer brought much grief to many who heard it. He said, "Because I am a Baptist." On every other question put to him during that question and answer session, he answered, "Because the Word of God says...." When we consistently seek to acknowledge and uphold the authority of God's Word, we will find unity, but when we switch from this authority to maintain our preferences, we will create disunity. Our response to this dear brother is not to prove him right or wrong, but to weep over the lack of sufficient appeal to scriptural authority and the pain and division it inevitably brings to the body of Christ.

Therefore, in our attempt to discover the God-ordained message of baptism, let us appeal solely to God's Word. A variety of messages regarding baptism flow out of the numerous denominational and extra-biblical sources available, but what does the Bible say? Without reference to any particular context, the Greek words for *baptism* could refer to washing, drowning, dipping, pouring, immersing, sprinkling, rinsing, cleansing, and other things. Since there are a variety of options, we must allow the author of Scripture to interpret his own words. We must resist choosing a meaning we are comfortable with and then forcing it upon the scriptural references to baptism.

To discover the right answer, we must study the words of Christ. Studies of extra-biblical sources can be both interesting and helpful at times, but they do not necessarily give us the sense of how Jesus used the term *baptism*. The Bible speaks often enough about baptism that we have more than enough information to discern what God means by it without using outside sources. In each case where the word *baptism* is found in Scripture, the surrounding context should be allowed to define its meaning.

Christ has commissioned us to be involved in the baptism of his church. He said, "Go therefore and make disciples of all nations, baptizing them in the name of the Father and the Son and the Holy Spirit" (Matt. 28:19). In one sense, all believers are baptists in the sense that we hold to the practice of baptizing and being baptized in obedience to Christ's command. But why did Jesus give us this command? What was the message he wanted us to communicate and receive through baptism?

Though we could wade deep into the Greek or Hebrew words for baptism to establish assumptions regarding its meaning, let me seek to speak simply. Regardless of what Bible translation we use, we will find reference to Naaman dipping himself into the Jordan River seven times to be cleansed of leprosy (2 Kings 5:10, 13, 14). When the Hebrew word here is translated into Greek, the translators will be most comfortable with the same word used in the New Testament Greek from which we get our references to baptism. In this sense, Naaman is baptizing himself seven times and does so by *dipping*, which some believe means total immersion, while others believe Naaman had himself ceremonially sprinkled. Whether or not he went all the way under the water of the Jordan is left unclear by the text.

Assume what you will for a moment. In Leviticus 11:32, the same word more plainly refers to an immersion when different articles are said to be put into water to become clean. If you are looking for a verse to prove the word for baptism can mean immersion, this would be a good text. It is interesting that the method for cleansing a leper (remember that Naaman was a leper in search of cleansing) in Leviticus 14:6-7, 51, refers to both dipping and then to taking what is dipped and sprinkling it seven times. It would be difficult to think the priests were required to take the living bird in this passage and completely immerse it in the blood of the slain bird. It is more practical to think one only needed to dip the bird deep enough to get the sprinkling effect described. Since Naaman was a leper seeking cleansing, it would seem that complete immersion would not have been required by the law for cleansing lepers. The main point is this: the words of these Old Testament passages can imply immersion, but they certainly do not require immersion. And when they seem to indicate the possibility of immersion, we have to infer that from other aspects of the context and not from the actual word for baptism alone.

For those who want to study this matter further, there are approximately seventeen references in the Old Testament that use the Hebrew word (טבל) which we translate into Greek as baptism (βάπτω). For example, in Leviticus 16:15-16, the priest is to dip (a baptism) his finger into the oil that was poured into the palm of his hand and then sprinkle the oil (a baptism by both dipping and sprinkling). In Ruth 2:14, Ruth is to dip (baptize) her bread into vinegar. Jonathan dips (baptizes) the end of his staff into a honeycomb to get some honey (1 Sam. 14:27). God has left us more examples like these, and they all provide a consistent understanding that the word for baptism does not always mean total immersion as some have been led to believe. Only in Leviticus 11:32 does it even seem natural to require total immersion.

There is no need to deny that there are words in the Bible that can describe immersion, and I have given examples. It must be understood, however, that these biblical words can in no way always mean, or even necessarily always imply, immersion. Any believers who look at all the biblical texts on baptism and seek to interpret them rightly will come to a like-minded conclusion. For centuries, believers have been divided over the meaning and mode of baptism. The only reason this division continues is our failure to observe all the evidence and then honestly submit to it.

Baptism in 1 Corinthians 10:2

> For I do not want you to be unaware, brethren, that our fathers were all under the cloud and all passed through the sea; and all were baptized into Moses in the cloud and in the sea (10:1-2).

When we read that "all were baptized into Moses in the cloud and in the sea," the word *baptized* obviously cannot mean *immersed* under water, since the text tells us the people referred to passed through the water on dry ground. This becomes quite evident when this passage is studied in its Old Testament context (Exod. 13:21; 14:22). The baptism referred to here is a dry ground baptism. All of Israel (infants included) were baptized into Moses. There is no mention of or reference to them being sprinkled, dipped, covered over with water, or buried in a watery grave, and yet God calls it a baptism. Israel was never immersed in the pillar of cloud or in the sea. The cloud went before them by day, and the sea parted for them to pass through on dry ground (Exod. 14:16, 21-22, 29). It was the Egyptians who were immersed in the sea, not Israel. Israel was baptized into Moses—a spiritual union. In other words, Israel was *united* by a covenant relationship with Moses through experiencing the cloud of God and the parting of the sea.

It is the word *baptized* that is used to describe this covenantal union. Any attempt to say that baptism always means *immersion* or *sprinkling* in this context destroys the intended meaning of God for this passage. The idea of being *united to* is much more synonymous with the biblical use (not cultural use) of the word baptized than the idea of being immersed or sprinkled. As an interesting note, the biblical symbolism in this text associated with immersion is that of judgment and not blessing. The Egyptians were immersed (Exod. 14:28) and the wicked inhabitants of the earth in Noah's day were also immersed. These biblical examples of immersion provide a sign of judgment rather than a sign of blessing; and yet when we baptize we are conveying blessing. To use the mode of immersion as God uses it in the Noahic flood and with the Egyptians is to use a sign of judgment as opposed to a sign of beauty and benefit. This should cause us at least a little concern if we choose immersion for the way we do the baptism God requires. Are there any non-judgmental references to baptism in Scripture that expressly and fully reveal participants completely covered over with water?

Baptism in 1 Corinthians 12:13

> For by one Spirit we were all baptized into one body, whether Jews or Greeks, whether slaves or free, and we were all made to drink of one Spirit.

"By one Spirit we were all baptized into one body" is another passage of Scripture demonstrating the message behind God's use of the word baptism—and it is not a message of immersion or any other mode. An immersed object does not generally become a part of what it is immersed into. If you immerse your hand into water, it becomes surrounded by water but does not become a part of the water. In this passage, God speaks about uniting people to the mystical body of Christ, not of simply surrounding them with this body. When we are baptized into the body of Christ, we actually become a part of it. We are united to it. Again, the idea of *union* is what God expresses when he discusses the baptism of his people.

Baptism in Acts 1:5

> ...for John baptized with water, but you will be baptized with the Holy Spirit not many days from now."

When Luke wrote that Jesus taught, "you shall be baptized with the Holy Spirit not many days from now," did this mean, "You shall be immersed in the Holy Spirit?" The best way to determine this is to study the passages of Scripture in which this verse is fulfilled and simply observe what actually took place. Acts 1:8 states "you will receive power when the Holy Spirit has *come upon* you" (emphasis added). In Acts 2:17, we have what was spoken of through the prophet Joel: "I will *pour forth* of my Spirit on all mankind" (emphasis added). Acts 10:44 says, "While Peter was still speaking these words, the Holy Spirit *fell upon* all those who were listening to the message" (emphasis added). And in Acts 11:15, "the Holy Spirit *fell upon* them just as He did upon us at the beginning" (emphasis added).

Though none of the above verses are meant to prove immersion, sprinkling, or pouring as the mode of baptism, they all clearly suggest that real spiritual baptism is not best symbolized by immersion since this is not what takes place. In each of these cases, the Greek verbs convey the idea of the Holy Spirit either "coming down upon," "pouring out upon," or "falling down upon." The message is that when we are baptized with the Holy Spirit, the Holy Spirit is the one who comes to us (not us to him) and he *unites* himself with us.

Baptism in Matthew 28:19

> Go therefore and make disciples of all the nations, baptizing them in the name of the Father and the Son and the Holy Spirit.

We have seen thus far that the meaning and message of baptism is wrapped in the concept of a union with God through Christ. This theme is no different in Matthew 28:19, where we find the words, "baptizing them in the name of the Father and the Son and the Holy Spirit." Here Christ institutes the sacrament of baptism as part of what is known as his Great Commission to the church. Having fulfilled the requirements of the new covenant through his death, burial, and resurrection, and now just before his ascension into heaven, Christ commissions his church to be regularly performing the work of baptizing. In the institution of this sacrament he places the ritual of baptism into a relationship with the triune God. The baptism was to be given to those who had received a new relationship with God by having become a disciple of Christ, and it was to be done in reference to and in union with God the Father, Son, and Holy Spirit.

Just as baptism meant a relationship with Moses for the Israelites when they were "baptized into Moses" (1 Cor. 10:2), and just as baptism meant a relationship with Paul for the Corinthians who were "baptized into the name of Paul" (1 Cor. 1:13), so baptism was to mean a union with the triune God when done according to the manner of Christ's Great Commission to the church.

Baptism in Romans 6:2-7

> May it never be! How shall we who died to sin still live in it? Or do you not know that all of us who have been *baptized* into Christ Jesus have been *baptized* into His death? Therefore we have been buried with Him through baptism into death, so that as Christ was raised from the dead through the glory of the Father, so we

> too might walk in newness of life. For if we have become *united* with Him in the likeness of His death, certainly we shall also be in the likeness of His resurrection, knowing this, that our old self was crucified with Him, in order that our body of sin might be done away with, so that we would no longer be slaves to sin; for he who has died is freed from sin (emphasis added).

Perhaps no passage speaks to the meaning or message of baptism more clearly than this one since it expressly uses *united* as a synonym for *baptized*. Here, God uses the concept of baptism to indicate the extent of our wonderful union with God through Christ's death, burial, and resurrection. A parallel passage to this one is Colossians 2:11-12, which similarly uses the phrase "buried with Him in baptism": "In Him you were also circumcised with a circumcision made without hands, in the removal of the body of the flesh by the circumcision of Christ; having been buried with Him in baptism, in which you were also raised up with Him through faith in the working of God, who raised Him from the dead." The emphasis here is that through baptism, or in our union with Christ, we are spiritually participants in all the benefits of Christ's death, burial, and resurrection. Our sinful nature is crucified and buried that we might be raised to new life and all of this through being united to Jesus Christ.

There are those who use the burial terminology of Romans 6 and Colossians 2 as support for thinking baptism means going all the way under water. This view brings the assumption of water to the text as opposed to finding it in the text. Neither of these passages mentions water. Neither say, "buried *by water*" into Christ. Why not? Because it is not the design of these texts to teach us about the *mode* of baptism: that is, how much water is to be used and the manner in which it is to be applied. Rather, these passages reveal the *meaning* of baptism. This is an important clarification often missed. If the word water was in the passage, it would teach baptismal regeneration, clearly an unbiblical doctrine. If immersionists imply water, they might be teaching much more than they are bargaining for. Without intending to or realizing it, they might be teaching baptismal regeneration, or the saving of a sinner by the ritual of baptism. The primary reason for the "death, burial, resurrection" terminology in the passage is because this is the terminology of the gospel: "For I delivered to you as of first importance what I also received, that Christ died for our sins according to the Scriptures, and that He was buried, and that He was raised on the third day according to the Scriptures" (1 Cor. 15:3-4). Paul is describing the gospel, our good news union with Christ. The "death, burial, resurrection" terminology demonstrates the ingredients of the gospel and not the ritual ingredients of baptism.

Furthermore, if the word *buried* only indicated immersion according to Romans 6:2-7, then it would contradict Galatians 3:27 where baptism indicates a "putting on" activity, not a "dunking down under" activity. Galatians 3:27 says, "For all of you who were baptized into Christ have clothed yourselves with Christ." For baptism to indicate one mode in one passage (say, immersion) and another mode in another passage (say, to be clothed, putting on) would be a contradiction in mode. In that case, the Galatians 3:27 passage would be teaching baptism participants that the proper way to be baptized would be by undressing and then dressing to achieve a picture of "being clothed with Christ," whereas Romans 6:2-7 would be teaching them that the proper way to be baptized would be by going all the way under water to achieve a picture of a western burial service. When the analogies of Romans 6 and Galatians 3 are rightly maintained as analogies, however, there is no contradiction since neither passage is meant to indicate the mode of baptism God has designed for us to employ. To attempt to teach the proper mode of baptism from either of these passages is to obscure the power of union with God through Christ being taught here. The purpose of both passages is the *meaning* of baptism as *union*, not how much water is used.

Let us not fail to see that we could just as easily choose the "being clothed" analogy in Galatians 3:27 for baptism as the "being buried" analogy in Romans 6:4. As a matter of fact, for several hundred years, parts of the early church practiced a naked baptism in favor of the Galatians 3:27 analogy. The baptism participants would come to baptism in their old clothes representing their old life polluted by sin. They would disrobe publicly and be washed by baptism to be purified from all their sin. Then they put on new clean clothes to symbolize being clothed in the righteousness of Christ. For the most part, the church has abandoned this service of baptism since many had difficulty with public nudity—especially when men were baptizing naked women. But as we have seen, the practice of naked baptism should have been abandoned because it was based on a passage that was never intended to teach us the mode of baptism. Good biblical interpretation always warns us from seeking to derive principles from analogies.

Where God speaks about the *mode* of baptism, he speaks of water or some other symbol for cleansing. But when God speaks about the *meaning* of baptism, he speaks about our relationship of union with him through the new covenant in Christ. He does not obscure the mode of baptism with the meaning of baptism. Neither should we. When we approach a text of Scripture on baptism we need to ask ourselves the question, "Is God's primary intention with this passage to teach us about the mode of baptism or the meaning of baptism?"

In Romans 6:2-7 three terms are used to indicate the extent of our union with Christ: *crucified*, *buried*, and *raised*. All three terms are designed to teach the same thing: a benefit through union with Christ. If we are united to Christ, then our sin should be crucified (mortified), buried (put away), and we should be walking in a new life (a resurrection life). That is the meaning of this passage. It is plainly not teaching anything about the mode of baptism. The word *baptism* is used here for its strong meaning of union with Christ. Notice that in the fifth verse God uses the word *united* as the most appropriate synonym for what is meant by *baptism*.

To insert "immersion under water" into the text of Romans 6 causes a number of imagery issues, not to mention textual issues: (1) Someone says, "I like immersion under water because immersion best symbolizes being united to Christ's death." But Christ died on a cross, not under water. Immersion doesn't really symbolize Christ's death, does it? (2) Someone else says, "I like immersion under water because immersion best symbolizes being buried with Christ." But Christ was buried in a cave on top of the ground. And he stayed buried for three days, not for a brief moment. How does immersion into and under water quickly enough so as not to drown someone symbolize this? (3) Another person says, "I like immersion under water because immersion best symbolizes being raised with Christ." But Christ arose from the dead by passing through the wound linen cloth, leaving it apparently undisturbed (John 20:6-7). How does coming up out of water dripping wet and hair all disturbed symbolize this?

Are we not guilty of superimposing a westernized modern day burial service upon the biblical record of the way Christ was actually crucified, buried, and raised? When the biblical description of Christ's death, burial, and resurrection is presented, the symbol of immersion under water fails to do what the immersionists want it to do. Furthermore, it distorts the correct interpretation of Scripture.

Romans 6:2-7 does not teach that baptism symbolizes the death, burial, and resurrection of Christ. What it teaches is that if we have been spiritually baptized into Christ (not ritually baptized with water), then such a union with him should automatically lead us to shun all sin. It is unthinkable that we would continue in sin, for such a union with Christ is a union into his death, burial, and resurrection. Christ was crucified, buried, and raised to put an end to the reign of sin in our lives. Our union with Christ (or our spiritual baptism into Christ) implies that we should be through with sin. Our sin should be crucified and buried. Our lives should be radically new because they are raised with Christ and have his resurrection power of victory over sin. We should no longer "continue in sin that grace might increase" (Rom. 6:1).

Think back to the time the lunar module docked with the mother ship and secured all the benefits of the mother ship for the crew inside the module. The docking procedure was televised and America watched with much concern because we knew that if the lunar module did not dock with the mother space ship, then all of the crew members in the module would perish. Once united to the mother ship, they received all of the life support systems the ship contained. Just so, when we are baptized into Christ, we are united to all the benefits that he secured for us by going to the cross, dying for us, being buried for us, and being raised for us. Without such union we perish, but with such a grace connection we are never again under bondage to sin. The domain of sin has been radically severed and left behind, just like the lunar module. We are now set free to new and glorious living and we are united to all the benefits secured by Christ's righteousness.

It is important not to obscure or distort the meaning of baptism in Romans 6 with assumptions about the mode. This passage shows the glorious extent of our separation from sin through union to God through Christ. Being united to Christ, we are united to all aspects of his work. Our sin has been destroyed and buried and we have risen to a new life. It is tragic when the mode of baptism is forced upon this text and this glorious message is covered and lost.

Now that we have discerned the biblical meaning of baptism, we are prepared to move forward into a discussion of the biblical mode and visible sign of baptism which consistently complements its meaning. If we let the Scripture renew our minds instead of being squeezed into cultural and religious molds, then we associate baptism with *union* (not sprinkling or pouring or immersion)—because that is the primary association God gives it. I know this creates a lack of clarity for some of us on how a child might have a genuine union with Christ in baptism. Answers to this issue are provided in the texts of Scripture and addressed later in this work. Difficult concepts from God require much patience in study and meditation while seeking submission to God's truth.

A Beautiful Message of Union

We have seen from Romans 6 and other Scripture that baptism first and foremost refers to a spiritual union with Christ. The glorious message of our union to God through Christ is beautiful and beneficial. The matter of baptism, however, can mean more than a spiritual union, for when water is applied it may refer to a ritual union. As a ritual union, baptism is both a sign and a seal.

As a sign, it is an advertisement of genuine union with Christ. God has given us the ritual of baptism to excite our senses with the glorious grace of being united with God the Father, Son, and Holy Spirit. As a seal, baptism confirms and authenticates all the benefits that come with the grace of union with our God. We should be clear that baptism as a seal does not produce the grace of salvation. Salvation is by grace through faith and repentance, and without God's gracious gifts of faith and repentance, it is impossible to be saved. Jesus said, "I tell you, no, but unless you repent, you will all likewise perish" (Luke 13:3), and as Paul wrote, "For by grace you have been saved through faith; and that not of yourselves, it is the gift of God; not as a result of works, so that no one may boast" (Eph. 2:8-9).

We cannot save ourselves or our children, or anyone else, by putting them through the ritual of baptism. Like the rainbow in the sky confirms God's promise never again to aim his wrath at his people (a sign that confirms God's gracious benefits but does not guarantee our election), so the ritual of baptism confirms that we have all the benefits of Christ through union with Christ, though it does not confer or guarantee election to eternal life. Baptism is a sign of the truth of our union with Christ and a seal of the benefits that come with that real union with Christ, but the benefits are only ours when that real union has occurred (not necessarily when the ritual occurs).

Where do we get the expression "sign and seal"? The language is used in Scripture in reference to circumcision. "And he received the *sign* of circumcision, a *seal* of the righteousness of the faith which he had while uncircumcised, so that he might be the father of all who believe without being circumcised, that righteousness might be credited to them" (Rom. 4:11, emphasis added). The language here refers us back to the language of Genesis 17:11, where circumcision is called "the sign of the covenant": "And you shall be circumcised in the flesh of your foreskin, and it shall be the sign of the covenant between Me and you." The sign and seal add nothing to what God does. They are for our benefit in understanding God's grace. They point out to us the union God has created in Christ, and give us confidence that such a wonderful union can really be ours. Baptism is not a badge or "feather in our cap" pointing to something we have done. It is a token of God's grace to his people—the beautiful and beneficial grace of union through Christ!

Remember back to the deliverance of the Jews under King Ahasuerus (Esther 8-9). The king's decree was sealed with his signet ring, which means that after the decree was written, wax was poured onto it and the ring of the king was then pressed into the wax before it cooled so that anyone examining the document at a later time would know it had the authority and blessing of the king upon it. The seal conveyed the intent of the king to honor all the promises written in the document upon the required conditions being met.

Like the seal on such a document, the seal of baptism can be applied long before the conditions of the covenant made in baptism are met. In baptism as in circumcision, God promised to extend to us all the blessings of his covenant through our faith in him as our God. Our faith does not force God to do anything or cause God to bless us. God blesses us according to his own will and his own pleasure (Eph. 1:7-11). By faith, we receive and embrace the blessings God provides by his grace and promises with his seal. Baptism is the beautiful seal of God received when faith in Christ is exercised. At that time, all the blessings God promises are poured out. We gloriously worship God in baptism because through baptism God has rich blessings for his people—the blessings through union with Christ, of which baptism is a sign and seal.

Discussion and Study Questions

1. How is determining our final and ultimate authority on the subject of baptism important to agree upon in reaching purity and unity in the body of Christ?
2. What can the words used in the Bible for *baptism* mean without reference to context? (There are eight or more options.) What is required of God's people to avoid inaccurate conclusions about the meaning of the word *baptism*?

3. What Old Testament texts might we use to prove that the word for baptism can mean dipping, sprinkling, or immersion? What do we make of the author's assumption that believers who look at all the biblical texts on baptism and seek to interpret them rightly will come to a like-minded conclusion?
4. In the 1 Corinthians 10:2 passage, Old Testament saints are described as having been baptized without water while the Egyptians were being judged with water through God's immersion of them into the Red Sea. Are there any non-judgmental references to baptism in Scripture that expressly reveal participants completely covered over with water?
5. It seems logical that the mode of baptism be consistent with the message of baptism, but what is the message (not mode) conveyed when God discusses the baptism of his people? How do we communicate this to young children?
6. Why is it that the unbiblical doctrine of baptismal regeneration might gain ground if one inserted the ritual of water baptism into the Romans 6:2-7 passage?
7. Since Galatians 3:27 provides a "being clothed" analogy for baptism while the Romans 6:4 passage uses a "being buried" analogy, why do many churches present only the concept of baptism as being buried with Christ? How might more instruction from Galatians 3:27 provide a better view of what God wants us to know about baptism in Christ?
8. Would it be safe to assume that whenever God seeks to teach us about baptism, he teaches us both about its meaning and mode? Why or why not? What general principle might we follow to ensure we do not obscure the mode of baptism with the meaning of baptism?

Chapter 3

The Beauty and Benefits of the Right Mode

I WAS TRAVELING to my in-laws for Christmas when I saw a highway billboard which read, "It's not that complicated ...One Lord, One Faith, One Baptism," signed, "God." Because this billboard contains the words of Ephesians 4:5, there is obviously truth here. There is but one baptism. But can you perform this one baptism more than one way? What about the passages of Scripture that say John, Jesus, Philip, and the Ethiopian eunuch went down into and came up out of the water? Does this not reveal the method of immersion? Yet don't the various Old Testament baptisms spring forward into the New Testament to reveal a method of sprinkling and pouring? There are obviously more than just a few Scripture references for this mode which need to be considered.

Two very different approaches are used on how God would want us to apply the sign of baptism. One approach is to rely heavily upon the etymology of the word *baptism*. How has the word been used and defined by those who have used it through its history? There are preachers who proclaim and books that cite dictionary after dictionary, or one author after another who says baptism *means* immersion—and so that is what it means. This meaning is then brought to the Scriptures as a tool to explain the texts of Scripture. We have already shown that the meaning of baptism as revealed in Scripture has to do with our covenant union with God through Christ. Nevertheless, even though the word *baptism* may mean something other than immersion, we should not be opposed to the mode of immersion if that is what our Lord teaches.

Another approach to discerning how to apply the sign of baptism is to postpone regard for etymology when biblical exegesis can be shown to clearly define God's meaning of the word baptism and his method for its application. Since God's Word (the Bible) is not only inerrant and infallible, and our only divine rule for faith and practice, it is sufficient to clarify all matters of faith without reliance upon extra-biblical sources. The exegetical or explanatory approach is the one employed here.

What is the biblical mode of baptism? For those willing to study, Scripture references abound on this subject. We do not need stacks of dictionaries or a multitude of human testimonies to look into this; we can investigate only the Bible for direction on how we should baptize. I believe the conclusion to such a study will show that the right administration of baptism is by the sprinkling or pouring of water in the name of the Father, Son, and Holy Spirit onto those who are professing believers in Christ and their children. This statement may sound presumptuous, even arrogant, without sufficient study. The amount of Scripture material applying to this matter is so great that only a few have truly taken the time for a thorough evaluation. They study enough to make some preliminary conclusions, but not enough to verify that their conclusions are consistent with every area of the Bible. We must be patient and withhold conclusions until we have investigated all the biblical references and facts.

I have listed here nine reasons for the mode of sprinkling and/or pouring which, when understood, blossoms with beauty and encourages and nurtures the church.

John the Baptist Demonstrates the Sprinkling Mode

Where did the practice of baptism begin? How did the Jews know of the transition from circumcision to baptism? Baptism had been prophesied in the Old Testament and was introduced in the

New Testament through John the Baptist. Many have assumed that John baptized by immersion, but the Gospels do not support such a view. Both John and his father were priests, and they baptized by sprinkling water and blood. It is reasonable to assume, if assumptions are to be made, that John would baptize in the same way as other priests. And he would also baptize in fulfillment of the prophecy of Ezekiel: "Then I will sprinkle clean water on you, and you will be clean; I will cleanse you from all your filthiness and from all your idols" (36:25). Let us specifically consider the examination of John the Baptist's baptizing by the Jews.

> And this is the witness of John, when the Jews sent to him priests and Levites from Jerusalem to ask him, "Who are you?" And he confessed, and did not deny, and he confessed, "I am not the Christ." And they asked him, "What then? Are you Elijah?" And he said, "I am not." "Are you the Prophet?" And he answered, "No." They said then to him, "Who are you, so that we may give an answer to those who sent us? What do you say about yourself?" He said, "I am a voice of one crying in the wilderness, 'Make straight the way of the Lord,' as Isaiah the prophet said." Now they had been sent from the Pharisees. And they asked him, and said to him, "Why then are you baptizing, if you are not the Christ, nor Elijah, nor the Prophet?"
>
> —John 1:19-25

In this passage, the Jews (priests and Levities) give no hint that John the Baptist was engaged in any new practice—which would be the case if he were immersing people. These Jews were from the Pharisees, referred to by some as "the eagle-eyed heresy hunters." Had John been doing something unacceptable, they would have made it known. Consequently, John's practice of baptism was not an issue with these Jews. Their questioning was not regarding John's practice but rather about who he was. Why did these students of God's word assume that John might be, in fulfillment of biblical prophecies, Christ, Elijah, or the Prophet? Obviously, there must be some Old Testament reference to Christ, Elijah, or the Prophet coming to baptize, because John had come on the scene doing just that. The Jews couldn't figure out why he would be baptizing if he was not Christ or Elijah or the Prophet. It is clear from their statements that they expected one of the distinguishing characteristics of the Messiah or the Prophet would be his work of baptizing. ("Why then are you baptizing if you are not the Christ, nor Elijah, nor the Prophet?") Since John was baptizing, then he must be, or at least he might be, the fulfillment of the biblical prophecies they knew so well.

Is it predicted that Christ, or Elijah, or the Prophet would come immersing anyone? Is it predicted that they will come sprinkling anyone? Whichever way the prediction goes is clearly the way John was baptizing since they saw the act of baptizing John practiced and associated him with Christ, Elijah, and the Prophet. When we research the Scriptures we see that all three (Christ, Elijah, and the Prophet) are associated with coming into the new covenant age sprinkling God's people. Thus, John the Baptist baptized by sprinkling because, if not, the questions the Jews asked him would not have been about him, but about why he was performing baptism incorrectly.

The Prophets Foretell a Sprinkling and Pouring Mode

Where then is it predicted that Christ or Elijah or the Prophet would come sprinkling?

> Behold, My servant will prosper, He will be high and lifted up, and greatly exalted. Just as many were astonished at you, My people, So His appearance was marred more than any man, And His form more than the sons of men. Thus He will *sprinkle* many nations, Kings will shut their mouths on account of Him; For what had not been told them they will see, And what they had not heard they will understand.
>
> —Isa. 52:13-15 emphasis added

> Then I will *sprinkle* clean water on you, and you will be clean; I will cleanse you from all your filthiness and from all your idols. Moreover, I will give you a new heart and put a new spirit within

> you; and I will remove the heart of stone from your flesh and give you a heart of flesh. And I will put my Spirit within you and cause you to walk in My statutes, and you will be careful to observe my ordinances.
>
> —Ezek. 36:25-27, emphasis added

Had John been baptizing using any other mode of baptism than that expressly described in the Old Testament prophets, the Jews would have had no logical basis for assuming John was the Messiah, the Prophet, or Elijah. The Old Testament Jew was expecting a baptism by sprinkling with the coming Messiah. They recognized John as doing something they had read about in Scripture, specifically in Isaiah 52:15 and Ezekiel 36:25.

There are some translations that either contend in their text or suggest in their margin notes that Isaiah 52:15 should be translated, "He will *startle* the nations" instead of, "He will *sprinkle* the nations." We should oppose such a translation for three reasons. First, the word *sprinkle* is consistent with the context in drawing out the unexpected work of the Messiah with a significant antithesis. He who himself would be marred in appearance more than any man, thus in a state of being ceremonially unclean, is the very one who will cleanse (sprinkle) the nations. The one who appears impure is the very one who will purify his people from their sins. (Old Testament purification ceremonies were frequently performed by sprinkling clean water.) This is one of the primary themes of Isaiah 52 and 53.

Second, the word *sprinkle* is the Hebrew word *nazah* and is found in twenty-three other places in Scripture. Without exception, every time the word is used it is translated "sprinkle." It is applied to the sprinkling of blood with the finger on the day of atonement (Lev. 16:14-15, 19), to water for cleansing or purification of lepers with a bunch of hyssop (Lev. 14:7), and to the ashes and water mixture of a red heifer upon those defiled through touching a corpse (Num. 19:17-18). The plain usage of the language strongly favors no other translation than *sprinkle*.

Third, the word *sprinkle* in Isaiah 52:15 provides the clearest association of baptism with the coming Messiah of any passage in the Old Testament. If this passage is eliminated as a source from which the Jews questioning John the Baptist could have learned the baptizing characteristics of the Messiah, then where else in the Old Testament could they have made such a certain deduction? The passage in Ezekiel refers to the practice of sprinkling coming with the messianic age, but only Isaiah clearly links the sprinkling function to the Messiah himself.

We recall that the Jews also allowed for the fact that John the Baptist might be "the Prophet" as a result of his baptizing (John 1:25). This prophet is predicted in Deuteronomy 18:15-19:

> The Lord your God will raise up for you a prophet like me from among you, from your countrymen, you shall listen to him. This is according to all that you asked of the Lord your God in Horeb on the day of the assembly, saying, 'Let me not hear again the voice of the Lord my God, let me not see this great fire anymore, or I will die.' The Lord said to me, 'they have spoken well. I will raise up a prophet from among their countrymen like you, and I will put My words in his mouth, and he shall speak to them all that I command him. It shall come about that whoever will not listen to My words which he shall speak in My name, I Myself will require it of him.

Though nothing is said of this prophet baptizing in any manner, he is described as being "like me." In other words, a prophet like Moses. Was Moses ever found baptizing as John the Baptist was doing? Moses was constantly engaged in "sprinkling." "For when every commandment had been spoken by Moses to all the people according to the Law, he took the blood of the calves and the goats, with water and scarlet wool and hyssop, and sprinkled both the book itself and all the people" (Heb. 9:19). If the prophet who was to come had functions like Moses, it could be expected that he would likewise be engaged in sprinkling as a sign of the "blood of the covenant which God commanded you" (Heb. 9:20).

The Jews questioning John the Baptist were looking for the Messianic King and the kingdom. They knew from thorough Old Testament study that one of the signs of this king and kingdom was sprinkling with water. Ezekiel wrote, "I will sprinkle clean water on you, and you will be clean; I will cleanse you from all your filthiness and from all your idols" (Ezek. 36:25). Since John the Baptist had come on the scene sprinkling water, then it was right for them to assume he was either Christ (Isa. 52:15), the Prophet (Deut. 18:15-19), or Elijah (Mal. 4:5; Matt. 11:14). The practice of Elijah was not to immerse but to pour—he poured water on his Mt. Carmel offering rather than immersing the wood into it; and he was to purify the sons of Levi (Mal. 3:3). Priests regularly practiced ritual purification by sprinkling. Had John been immersing instead of sprinkling, the Jews would not have had any basis for questioning who he was, and they would not have mistaken him for Christ, the Prophet, or Elijah.

I was once a lookout for a surprise birthday party, charged to watch out for the birthday boy's approach. When I discovered him coming, I was to notify the party participants to get into hiding. But I didn't know what the birthday boy looked like. After sharing my lack of qualifications for the lookout position, I was informed that all I had to do was to look for two characteristics of the birthday boy: "He will be driving his Ford Mustang and wearing a baseball cap—he always wears a baseball cap." Before long, I saw a Mustang coming down the road and what looked like someone wearing a hat. I promptly told everyone to get ready for our celebrated person's arrival. Well, it wasn't him, even though the driver was wearing a cap and the automobile he was driving was a Mustang. He had the characteristics I was told to look for, but I identified the wrong boy. In the same way, it is easy to see why the Pharisees said what they did concerning John the Baptist. He had the characteristic they were told by God's Word to be on the lookout for, and that was a baptism by sprinkling.

The Jews and John's Disciples Understood a Sprinkling Mode

> Therefore there arose a discussion on the part of John's disciples with a Jew about purification. And they came to John and said to him, "Rabbi, He who was with you beyond the Jordan, to whom

> you have testified, behold, He is baptizing and all are coming to Him.
>
> —John 3:25-26

How did the Jews understand John's baptism? This passage from the gospel of John would indicate that they understood it to be some form of purification. Their discussion was about purification, and how was purification normally observed and performed for the Jews? By sprinkling and pouring.

> *To cleanse* the house then, he shall take two birds and cedar wood and a scarlet string and hyssop, and he shall slaughter the one bird in an earthenware vessel over running water. Then he shall take the cedar wood and the hyssop and the scarlet string, with the live bird, and dip them in the blood of the slain bird as well as in the running water, and *sprinkle* the house seven times.
>
> —Lev. 14:49-51 emphasis added

> Again the Lord spoke to Moses, saying, "Take the Levites from among the sons of Israel and cleanse them. Thus you shall do to them, *for their cleansing: sprinkle purifying water on them,* and let them use a razor over their whole body and wash their clothes, and they will be clean."
>
> —Num. 8:5-7 emphasis added

> Anyone who touches a corpse, the body of a man who has died, and does not *purify* himself, defiles the tabernacle of the Lord; and that person shall be cut off from Israel. Because *the water for impurity was not sprinkled* on him, he shall be unclean; his uncleanness is still on him.
>
> —Num. 19:13 emphasis added

Since John was a priest, the Jews considered his baptism a legal and rightful form of purification and cleansing. This discussion was not about any new immersion method for purification, which should have occurred if John was performing purification in an uncharacteristic manner. The concern to the Jews was over the transition from John "doing purification" (baptizing) and Jesus beginning to attract larger crowds than John and baptizing them. John was pleased with the transition since he knew "He must increase, but I must decrease" (John 3:30). When John saw Jesus he declared, "Behold, the Lamb of God who takes away the sin of the world!" (John 1:29). Such a declaration would not have made sense without an understanding from the Old Testament of our need for purification through union with Christ, a purification signified outwardly through a baptism of sprinkling clean water.

The Early Church Was Accustomed to Worship which Included a Sprinkling Mode

> The Holy Spirit is signifying this, that the way into the holy place has not yet been disclosed while the outer tabernacle is still standing, which is a symbol for the present time. Accordingly both gifts and sacrifices are offered which cannot make the worshiper perfect in conscience, since they relate only to food and drink and various washings [*various baptisms*], regulations for the body imposed until a time of reformation. But when Christ appeared as a high priest of the good things to come, He entered through the greater and more perfect tabernacle, not made with hands, that is to say, not of this creation; and not through the blood of goats and calves, but through His own blood, He entered the holy place once for all, having obtained eternal redemption. For if the blood of goats and bulls and the ashes of a heifer *sprinkling* those who have been defiled sanctify for the cleansing of the flesh, how much more will the blood of Christ, who through the eternal Spirit offered Himself without blemish to God, cleanse your conscience from dead works to serve the living God? For this reason He is the mediator of a new covenant, so that, since a death has taken place for the redemption of the transgressions that were committed under the first covenant, those who have been called may receive the promise of the eternal inheritance. For where a covenant is, there must of necessity be the death of the one who made it. For a covenant is valid only when men are dead, for it is never in force while the one who made it lives. Therefore even the first covenant was not inaugurated without blood. For when every commandment had been spoken by Moses to all the people according to the Law, he took the blood

> of the calves and the goats, with water and scarlet wool and hyssop, and *sprinkled* both the book itself and all the people, saying, "THIS IS THE BLOOD OF THE COVENANT WHICH GOD COMMANDED YOU." And in the same way he *sprinkled* both the tabernacle and all the vessels of the ministry with the blood. And according to the Law, one may almost say, all things are cleansed with blood, and without shedding of blood there is no forgiveness. Therefore it was necessary for the copies of the things in the heavens to be cleansed with these, but the heavenly things themselves with better sacrifices than these.
>
> —Heb. 9:8-23, emphasis added

What a wonderful passage demonstrating how Jesus Christ brings us a new and better covenant. But in the process of explaining this, the author of Hebrews also tells us much about the ritual service of the old covenant. Notice how the Jews were familiar with ritual baptisms by sprinkling and pouring. A regular part of their worship services involved participating in sprinklings. The people of God did not all of a sudden begin using water in their worship services in the New Testament. They were accustomed to using water as a symbol of being united to God through cleansing from sin. They were practically unable to attend a worship service in which they did not see a sprinkling. In Hebrews 9:10, the phrase "various washings" is a use of the Greek word *baptismois*. In other words, these various washings refer to "various baptisms." The Old Testament law never required immersions, but frequently required sprinklings. These sprinklings in the book of Hebrews are referred to as "various baptisms," and the various baptisms are performed by sprinkling. No other synonyms are used; there is no dipping, dunking, or immersing.

It is difficult to explain why all these different kinds of baptisms were by sprinkling if sprinkling is not held forth as the proper baptism mode. Sprinkling is an Old Testament requirement for baptism which the Jews and John the Baptist knew well, and this requirement continued from the Old Testament into the New Testament. Unless God provides specific instruction for the Jews to change the way they were doing things, it only makes sense that sprinkling continue as a visual sign for the church from God. Does God anywhere command his people to abandon his symbol of sprinkling in favor of a new symbol of immersing?

A Whole Bible Review Overwhelms Us with God's Love of a Sprinkling Mode

When the entire Bible is reviewed, it reveals God's clear affinity for sprinkling and pouring through a multitude of references. God wants us to know that he has designed worship to include these two elements. He expressly required this in the Old Testament, and numerous references show how this design of God carries over into the New Testament. (Those believers who have been raised in a "New Testament Only" tradition will find this to be a radically new insight into God's will.) God could have easily designed immersion practices to be included in both Old and New Testament worship if he had wanted. It should not seem strange that he never uses the word immerse, not even once, for God chose what he wanted and described it for us throughout the entirety of the Bible.

I have listed ninety-six of the biblical references to sprinkling and pouring that have some specific tie to the corporate worship of God's people. I have omitted references to God *pouring* out his wrath and anger, our individual times of *pouring* out our hearts in prayer, the soul being *poured* out within, clouds *pouring* out water, creation *pouring* forth speech, or blood being *sprinkled* in battle. The references I have chosen to list give us some sense of God's desire to have us understand that there is a pouring or sprinkling activity or symbol included in the proper worship of God. Why would God make his precepts and preferences for pouring and sprinkling so clear if some other mode like immersion was to be taught to us as the proper mode of baptism? With the clear pattern of sprinkling and pouring in the worship of the people of God, could those living in the Old Testament era or those living at the time of Christ imagine "going to church" and not seeing some form of sprinkling or pouring? To see an immersion would have been something radically new and would have required clear explanation.

So Jacob rose early in the morning, and took the stone that he had put under his head and set it up as a pillar, and *poured* oil on its top.

—Gen. 28:18

And Jacob set up a pillar in the place where He had spoken with him, a pillar of stone, and he *poured* out a libation on it; he also *poured* oil on it.

—Gen. 35:14

And Moses took half of the blood and put it in basins and the other half of the blood he *sprinkled* on the altar.

—Exod. 24:6

So Moses took the blood and *sprinkled* it on the people, and said, "Behold the blood of the covenant, which the Lord has made with you in accordance with all these words."

—Exod. 24:8

And you shall make its dishes and its pans and its jars and its bowls, with which to *pour* libations; you shall make them of pure gold.

—Exod. 25:29

Then you shall take the anointing oil, and *pour* it on his head and anoint him.

—Exod. 29:7

And you shall take some of the blood of the bull and put it on the horns of the altar with your finger; and you shall *pour* out all the blood at the base of the altar.

—Exod. 29:12

And you shall slaughter the ram and shall take its blood and *sprinkle* it around on the altar.

—Exod. 29:16

And you shall slaughter the ram, and take some of its blood and put it on the lobe of Aaron's right ear and on the lobes of his sons' right ears and on the thumbs of their right hands and on the big toes of their right feet, and *sprinkle* the rest of the blood around on the altar. Then you shall take some of the blood that is on the altar and some of the anointing oil, and *sprinkle it on* Aaron and on his garments, and on his sons and on his sons' garments with him; so he and his garments shall be consecrated, as well as his sons and his sons' garments with him.

—Exod. 29:20-21

You shall not offer any strange incense on this altar, or burnt offering or meal offering; and you shall not *pour* out a libation on it.

—Exod. 30:9

It shall not be *poured* on anyone's body, nor shall you make any like it, in the same proportions; it is holy, and it shall be holy to you.

—Exod. 30:32

And he made the utensils which were on the table, its dishes and its pans and its bowls and its jars, with which to *pour* out libations, of pure gold.

—Exod. 37:16

And he shall slay the young bull before the Lord; and Aaron's sons, the priests, shall offer up the blood and *sprinkle* the blood around on the altar that is at the doorway of the tent of meeting.

—Lev. 1:5

And he shall slay it on the side of the altar northward before the Lord, and Aaron's sons, the priests, shall *sprinkle* its blood around on the altar.

—Lev. 1:11

Now when anyone presents a grain offering as an offering to the Lord, his offering shall be of fine flour, and he shall *pour* oil on it and put frankincense on it.

—Lev. 2:1

You shall break it into bits, and *pour* oil on it; it is a grain offering.
—Lev. 2:6

And he shall lay his hand on the head of his offering and slay it at the doorway of the tent of meeting, and Aaron's sons, the priests, shall *sprinkle* the blood around on the altar.
—Lev. 3:2

And he shall lay his hand on the head of his offering, and slay it before the tent of meeting; and Aaron's sons shall *sprinkle* its blood around on the altar.
—Lev. 3:8

And he shall lay his hand on its head and slay it before the tent of meeting; and the sons of Aaron shall *sprinkle* its blood around on the altar.
—Lev. 3:13

And the priest shall dip his finger in the blood, and *sprinkle* some of the blood seven times before the Lord, in front of the veil of the sanctuary. 'the priest shall also put some of the blood on the horns of the altar of fragrant incense which is before the Lord in the tent of meeting; and all the blood of the bull he shall *pour* out at the base of the altar of burnt offering which is at the doorway of the tent of meeting.
—Lev. 4:6-7

...that is, all the rest of the bull, he is to bring out to a clean place outside the camp where the ashes are *poured* out, and burn it on wood with fire; where the ashes are *poured* out it shall be burned.
—Lev. 4:12

And the priest shall dip his finger in the blood, and *sprinkle* it seven times before the Lord, in front of the veil. And he shall put some of the blood on the horns of the altar which is before the Lord in the tent of meeting; and all the blood he shall *pour* out at the base of the altar of burnt offering which is at the doorway of the tent of meeting.
—Lev. 4:17-18

Then the priest is to take some of the blood of the sin offering with his finger, and put it on the horns of the altar of burnt offering; and the rest of its blood he shall *pour* out at the base of the altar of burnt offering.

—Lev. 4:25

And the priest shall take some of its blood with his finger and put it on the horns of the altar of burnt offering; and all the rest of its blood he shall *pour* out at the base of the altar.

—Lev. 4:30

And the priest is to take some of the blood of the sin offering with his finger and put it on the horns of the altar of burnt offering; and all the rest of its blood he shall *pour* out at the base of the altar.

—Lev. 4:34

He shall also *sprinkle* some of the blood of the sin offering on the side of the altar, while the rest of the blood shall be drained out at the base of the altar: it is a sin offering.

—Lev. 5:9

In the place where they slay the burnt offering they are to slay the guilt offering, and he shall *sprinkle* its blood around on the altar.

—Lev. 7:2

And of this he shall present one of every offering as a contribution to the Lord; it shall belong to the priest who *sprinkles* the blood of the peace offerings.

—Lev. 7:14

And he *sprinkled* some of it on the altar seven times and anointed the altar and all its utensils, and the basin and its stand, to consecrate them. Then he *poured* some of the anointing oil on Aaron's head and anointed him, to consecrate him.

—Lev. 8:11-12

Next Moses slaughtered it and took the blood and with his finger put some of it around on the horns of the altar, and purified the altar. Then he *poured* out the rest of the blood at the base of the altar and consecrated it, to make atonement for it.

—Lev. 8:15

And Moses slaughtered it and *sprinkled* the blood around on the altar.

—Lev. 8:19

He also had Aaron's sons come near; and Moses put some of the blood on the lobe of their right ear, and on the thumb of their right hand, and on the big toe of their right foot. Moses then *sprinkled* the rest of the blood around on the altar.

—Lev. 8:24

So Moses took some of the anointing oil and some of the blood which was on the altar, and *sprinkled* it on Aaron, on his garments, on his sons, and on the garments of his sons with him; and he consecrated Aaron, his garments, and his sons, and the garments of his sons with him.

—Lev. 8:30

And Aaron's sons presented the blood to him; and he dipped his finger in the blood, and put some on the horns of the altar, and *poured* out the rest of the blood at the base of the altar.

—Lev. 9:9

Then he slaughtered the burnt offering; and Aaron's sons handed the blood to him and he *sprinkled* it around on the altar.

—Lev. 9:12

Then he slaughtered the ox and the ram, the sacrifice of peace offerings which was for the people; and Aaron's sons handed the blood to him and he *sprinkled* it around on the altar.

—Lev. 9:18

He shall then *sprinkle* seven times the one who is to be cleansed from the leprosy, and shall pronounce him clean, and shall let the live bird go free over the open field.

—Lev. 14:7

The priest shall also take some of the log of oil, and *pour* it into his left palm; the priest shall then dip his right-hand finger into the oil that is in his left palm, and with his finger *sprinkle* some of the oil seven times before the Lord.

—Lev. 14:15-16

The priest shall also *pour* some of the oil into his left palm; and with his right-hand finger the priest shall *sprinkle* some of the oil that is in his left palm seven times before the Lord.

—Lev. 14:26-27

Then he shall take the cedar wood and the hyssop and the scarlet string, with the live bird, and dip them in the blood of the slain bird, as well as in the running water, and *sprinkle* the house seven times.

—Lev. 14:51

Moreover, he shall take some of the blood of the bull and *sprinkle* it with his finger on the mercy seat on the east side; also in front of the mercy seat he shall *sprinkle* some of the blood with his finger seven times. Then he shall slaughter the goat of the sin offering which is for the people, and bring its blood inside the veil, and do with its blood as he did with the blood of the bull, and *sprinkle* it on the mercy seat and in front of the mercy seat.

—Lev. 16:14-15

And with his finger he shall *sprinkle* some of the blood on it seven times, and cleanse it, and from the impurities of the sons of Israel consecrate it.

—Lev. 16:19

And the priest shall *sprinkle* the blood on the altar of the Lord at the doorway of the tent of meeting, and offer up the fat in smoke as a soothing aroma to the Lord.

—Lev. 17:6

So when any man from the sons of Israel, or from the aliens who sojourn among them, in hunting catches a beast or a bird which may be eaten, he shall *pour* out its blood and cover it with earth.

—Lev. 17:13

And the priest who is the highest among his brothers, on whose head the anointing oil has been *poured*, and who has been consecrated to wear the garments, shall not uncover his head, nor tear his clothes.

—Lev. 21:10

The man shall then bring his wife to the priest, and shall bring as an offering for her one-tenth of an ephah of barley meal; he shall not *pour* oil on it, nor put frankincense on it, for it is a grain offering of jealousy, a grain offering of memorial, a reminder of iniquity.

—Num. 5:15

And thus you shall do to them, for their cleansing: *sprinkle* purifying water on them, and let them use a razor over their whole body, and wash their clothes, and they shall be clean.

—Num. 8:7

But the first-born of an ox or the first-born of a sheep or the first-born of a goat, you shall not redeem; they are holy. You shall *sprinkle* their blood on the altar and shall offer up their fat in smoke as an offering by fire, for a soothing aroma to the Lord.

—Num. 18:17

Next Eleazar the priest shall take some of its blood with his finger, and *sprinkle* some of its blood toward the front of the tent of meeting seven times.

—Num. 19:4

Anyone who touches a corpse, the body of a man who has died, and does not purify himself, defiles the tabernacle of the Lord; and that person shall be cut off from Israel. Because the water for impurity was not *sprinkled* on him, he shall be unclean; his uncleanness is still on him.

—Num. 19:13

And a clean person shall take hyssop and dip it in the water, and *sprinkle* it on the tent and on all the furnishings and on the persons who were there, and on the one who touched the bone or the one slain or the one dying naturally or the grave. Then the clean person shall *sprinkle* on the unclean on the third day and on the seventh day; and on the seventh day he shall purify him from uncleanness, and he shall wash his clothes and bathe himself in water and shall be clean by evening. But the man who is unclean and does not purify himself from uncleanness, that person shall be cut off from the midst of the assembly, because he has defiled the sanctuary of the Lord; the water for impurity has not been *sprinkled* on him, he is unclean. So it shall be a perpetual statute for them. And he who *sprinkles* the water for impurity shall wash his clothes, and he who touches the water for impurity shall be unclean until evening.

—Num. 19:18-21

Then the libation with it shall be a fourth of a hin for each lamb, in the holy place you shall *pour* out a libation of strong drink to the Lord.

—Num. 28:7

Only you shall not eat the blood; you are to *pour* it out on the ground like water.

—Deut. 12:16

You shall not eat it; you shall *pour* it out on the ground like water.

—Deut. 12:24

And you shall offer your burnt offerings, the flesh and the blood, on the altar of the Lord your God; and the blood of your sacrifices shall be *poured* out on the altar of the Lord your God, and you shall eat the flesh.

—Deut. 12:27

Only you shall not eat its blood; you are to *pour* it out on the ground like water.

—Deut. 15:23

And they took them from inside the tent and brought them to Joshua and to all the sons of Israel, and they *poured* them out before the Lord.

—Josh. 7:23

And the angel of God said to him, "Take the meat and the unleavened bread and lay them on this rock, and *pour* out the broth." And he did so.

—Judg. 6:20

And they gathered to Mizpah, and drew water and *poured* it out before the Lord, and fasted on that day, and said there, "We have sinned against the Lord." And Samuel judged the sons of Israel at Mizpah.

—1 Sam. 7:6

Then Samuel took the flask of oil, *poured* it on his head, kissed him and said, "Has not the Lord anointed you a ruler over His inheritance?

—1 Sam. 10:1

So the three mighty men broke through the camp of the Philistines, and drew water from the well of Bethlehem which was by the gate, and took it and brought it to David. Nevertheless he would not drink it, but *poured* it out to the Lord.

—2 Sam. 23:16

Then he gave a sign the same day, saying, "This is the sign which the Lord has spoken, 'Behold, the altar shall be split apart and the ashes which are on it shall be *poured* out.'"

—1 Kings 13:3

The altar also was split apart and the ashes were *poured* out from the altar, according to the sign which the man of God had given by the word of the Lord.

—1 Kings 13:5

Then he arranged the wood and cut the ox in pieces and laid it on the wood. And he said, "Fill four pitchers with water and *pour* it on the burnt offering and on the wood."

—1 Kings 18:33

But Jehoshaphat said, "Is there not a prophet of the Lord here that we may inquire of the Lord by him?" And one of the king of Israel's servants answered and said, "Elisha the son of Shaphat is here, who used to *pour* water on the hands of Elijah."

—2 Kings 3:11

Then take the flask of oil and *pour* it on his head and say, "Thus says the Lord," 'I have anointed you king over Israel.' Then open the door and flee and do not wait."

—2 Kings 9:3

And he arose and went into the house, and he *poured* the oil on his head and said to him, "Thus says the Lord, the God of Israel, 'I have anointed you king over the people of the Lord, even over Israel.'"

—2 Kings 9:6

And burned his burnt offering and his meal offering, and *poured* his libation and *sprinkled* the blood of his peace offerings on the altar.

—2 Kings 16:13

Then King Ahaz commanded Urijah the priest, saying, "Upon the great altar burn the morning burnt offering and the evening meal offering and the king's burnt offering and his meal offering, with the burnt offering of all the people of the land and their meal offering and their libations; and *sprinkle* on it all the blood of the burnt offering and all the blood of the sacrifice. But the bronze altar shall be for me to inquire by."

—2 Kings 16:15

So the three broke through the camp of the Philistines, and drew water from the well of Bethlehem which was by the gate, and took it and brought it to David; nevertheless David would not drink it, but *poured* it out to the Lord.

—1 Chron. 11:18

So they slaughtered the bulls, and the priests took the blood and *sprinkled* it on the altar. They also slaughtered the rams and *sprinkled* the blood on the altar; they slaughtered the lambs also and *sprinkled* the blood on the altar.

—2 Chron. 29:22

And they stood at their stations after their custom, according to the law of Moses the man of God; the priests *sprinkled* the blood which they received from the hand of the Levites.

—2 Chron. 30:16

And they slaughtered the Passover animals, and while the priests *sprinkled* the blood received from their hand, the Levites skinned them.

—2 Chron. 35:11

The sorrows of those who have bartered for another god will be multiplied; I shall not *pour* out their libations of blood, nor shall I take their names upon my lips.

—Ps. 16:4

Thus He will *sprinkle* many nations, Kings will shut their mouths on account of Him; for what had not been told them they will see, and what they had not heard they will understand.

—Isa. 52:15

Therefore, I will allot Him a portion with the great, And He will divide the booty with the strong; Because He *poured* out Himself to death, and was numbered with the transgressors; Yet He Himself bore the sin of many, And interceded for the transgressors.

—Isa. 53:12

Among the smooth stones of the ravine is your portion, they are your lot; Even to them you have *poured* out a libation, you have made a grain offering. Shall I relent concerning these things?

—Isa. 57:6

When I had brought them into the land which I swore to give to them, then they saw every high hill and every leafy tree, and they offered there their sacrifices, and there they presented the provocation of their offering. There also they made their soothing aroma, and there they *poured* out their libations.

—Ezek. 20:28

Then I will *sprinkle* clean water on you, and you will be clean; I will cleanse you from all your filthiness and from all your idols.

—Ezek. 36:25

"And I will not hide My face from them any longer, for I shall have *poured* out My Spirit on the house of Israel," declares the Lord God.

—Ezek. 39:29

And He said to me, "Son of man, thus says the Lord God, 'these are the statutes for the altar on the day it is built, to offer burnt offerings on it and to *sprinkle* blood on it.'"

—Ezek. 43:18

And he will make a firm covenant with the many for one week, but in the middle of the week he will put a stop to sacrifice and grain offering; and on the wing of abominations will come one who makes desolate, even until a complete destruction, one that is decreed, is *poured* out on the one who makes desolate.

—Dan. 9:2

They will not *pour* out libations of wine to the Lord. Their sacrifices will not please Him. Their bread will be like mourners' bread; all who eat of it will be defiled, For their bread will be for themselves alone; It will not enter the house of the Lord.

—Hosea 9:4

For this is My blood of the covenant, which is *poured* out for many for forgiveness of sins.

—Matt. 26:28

And He said to them, "This is My blood of the covenant, which is *poured* out for many."

—Mark 14:24

And in the same way He took the cup after they had eaten, saying, "This cup which is *poured* out for you is the new covenant in My blood.

—Luke 22:20

But even if I am being *poured* out as a drink offering upon the sacrifice and service of your faith, I rejoice and share my joy with you all.

—Phil. 2:17

For I am already being *poured* out as a drink offering, and the time of my departure has come.

—2 Tim. 4:6

Whom He *poured* out upon us richly through Jesus Christ our Savior.

—Titus 3:6

For if the blood of goats and bulls and the ashes of a heifer *sprinkling* those who have been defiled, sanctify for the cleansing of the flesh, ...

—Heb. 9:13

For when every commandment had been spoken by Moses to all the people according to the Law, he took the blood of the calves and the goats, with water and scarlet wool and hyssop, and *sprinkled* both the book itself and all the people.

—Heb. 9:19

And in the same way he *sprinkled* both the tabernacle and all the vessels of the ministry with the blood.

—Heb. 9:21

Let us draw near with a sincere heart in full assurance of faith, having our hearts *sprinkled* clean from an evil conscience and our bodies washed with pure water.

—Heb. 10:22

> By faith he kept the Passover and the *sprinkling* of the blood, so that he who destroyed the first-born might not touch them.
>
> —Heb. 11:28

> And to Jesus, the mediator of a new covenant, and to the *sprinkled* blood, which speaks better than the blood of Abel.
>
> —Heb. 12:24

> ...according to the foreknowledge of God the Father, by the sanctifying work of the Spirit, that you may obey Jesus Christ and be *sprinkled* with His blood: May grace and peace be yours in fullest measure.
>
> —1 Pet. 1:2

Scanning this list will show how common it was for the priest to lead the people of God in worship through pouring out blood and water and through sprinkling blood and water. Remember, God has given us this word for our instruction so that we might be thoroughly furnished for our work. "For whatever was written in earlier times was written for our instruction, so that through perseverance and the encouragement of the Scriptures we might have hope" (Rom. 15:4). "All Scripture is inspired by God and profitable for teaching, for reproof, for correction, for training in righteousness; so that the man of God may be adequate, equipped for every good work" (2 Tim. 3:16-17). Let us not be ignorant of God's frequent use of the sprinkling and pouring symbolism. This picture points us to the beauty and benefits of Christ. Over and over again, God told his people they needed to receive a pouring and a sprinkling from heaven to be fulfilled. They are only completely fulfilled when sanctified by the Holy Spirit and spiritually sprinkled with the blood of Jesus—"according to the foreknowledge of God the Father, by the sanctifying work of the Spirit, to obey Jesus Christ and be sprinkled with His blood: May grace and peace be yours in the fullest measure" (1 Pet. 1:2).

A Bible-Alone Approach Presents a Sprinkling Mode

The prophets and the people of the Bible practiced baptism by sprinkling. Since that is the case, one is obligated to assume that subsequent baptisms were and should be administered that way unless, of course, we can find reference to a command from God to change the practice he clearly began. Many immersionists will say they can prove that the origin of the Greek word for baptism only means *immersion*. But that is definitely not the only usage of the word, and the people of God should not be taught that it is. The Bible expressly refers to baptism as meaning union with Christ (Rom. 6:3-5), and it clearly reveals various baptisms being performed by sprinkling (Heb. 9:10, 13, 19, 21). Therefore, it is untrue to say the word for baptism only means immersion. It is even more disconcerting to assume, as many do, that the scriptural usage of baptism is somehow dependant on extra biblical or limited classical usage. What kind of Bible would we have if we had to depend on extra-biblical etymology to understand what God was saying? It is far better to trust God's Word as Spirit-inspired and totally sufficient as it stands without any need of additional sources to make it understandable or useful to us. As the apostle Paul wrote, "All Scripture is inspired by God and profitable for teaching, for reproof, for correction, for training in righteousness; so that the man of God may be adequate, equipped for every good work" (2 Tim. 3:16-17).

Imagine that you had never been to a church service or read any religious histories. Now imagine you have just been saved by the sovereign mercy of God, and that the one sharing the Good News of Christ with you gives you a Bible to read, which you do, cover to cover. Without any prior knowledge and without any dictionaries or encyclopedias, what would you say is the proper mode of baptism? In reading the Bible, you will never read the words immersion, dipped, or dunked in reference to the topic of baptism—not once. You will read of repeated examples of sprinkling and pouring, and you will also read that the Messiah and new covenant are ushered in with clean water sprinkled on the nations. You would note that the Jew was familiar with ritual baptisms by sprinkling and that Christ came to baptize the Jew first and then the Gentile. Wouldn't the Jew be quite confused with an immersion? If you are reading in the original Greek language of the New Testament, unaffected by translations, you will specifically read of "various baptisms," all occurring by sprinkling in the book of Hebrews. How would you come up with any mode other than sprinkling and pouring if all you had was the Bible? I acknowledge there are those who will take issue with this, and so I will consider their objections in the next chapter.

A Baptism for the Whole World Works with a Sprinkling or Pouring Mode

Sprinkling and pouring can be performed anywhere with anybody. This is not true of immersion. One of the tests we can employ for evaluating the rightness of our interpretation of Scripture is to consider its application among every tribe, tongue, and people group. The ultimate test, of course, is the consistency of God's Word: Scripture interprets Scripture. When we have investigated all of God's revelation on a subject and found the interpretation that leaves no references out of accord with the rest, then we should consider the application of these Scriptures. We never understand a doctrine of God rightly if we do not understand its application—"All Scripture is inspired by God and profitable" (2 Tim. 3:16).

If, for example, I am preaching a proper understanding of God's doctrine of prosperity, then it will take into account people of God who live in the many poor countries and tribal regions of the world. God told us to go to every ethnic group making his disciples, and after baptizing them we are to be teaching them everything he commanded (Matt. 28:19-20). In other words, we do not end up in some tribal region of Africa saying the portions of God's Word regarding prosperity need not be taught here because they just don't apply. Something is wrong if the Word for God's people does not fit the needs of God's people. We never need to change or ignore God's Word for it is infallible and without error and profitable for teaching, reproof, correction, and for training in righteousness. What we often need to change or adjust, however, is our interpretation.

I have fellowship almost weekly with a dear brother in Christ who prefers to baptize by immersion. But when he served the Lord in Alaska, he would sometimes find it impossible to do baptism in that manner. Finding enough unfrozen water for immersion when temperatures stayed below freezing for such long periods of time was difficult and often impossible. Didn't God consider the obstacles his people would face with baptism? Didn't he consider that when he told us to baptize every ethnic group he would be commanding us to baptize both in the weltering desert and in below freezing weather? Didn't he realize we would at times be baptizing the infirmed and bed-ridden, the large and the small, the young and the old? The scriptural mode of sprinkling and pouring can be performed in every climate, in every country, and on every person regardless of age or infirmity. This cannot be said of immersion. The Great Commission God gave us was to "Go therefore and make disciples of all the nations, baptizing them in the name of the Father and the Son and the Holy Spirit" (Matt. 28:19). God would not command what we could not by his grace perform. Baptism is an ordinance for the world, and as such, God has designed its application in such a way that every disciple may observe it and every pastor may perform it regardless of climate, season, or human ability.

The Baptism of Paul Best Fits a Sprinkling or Pouring Mode

> So Ananias departed and entered the house, and after laying his hands on him said, "Brother Saul, the Lord Jesus, who appeared to you on the road by which you were coming, has sent me so that you may regain your sight and be filled with the Holy Spirit." And immediately there fell from his eyes something like scales, and he regained his sight, and he got up and was baptized; and he took food and was strengthened.
>
> —Acts 9:17-19

This passage in Acts would indicate Paul's baptism occurred in the house of Judas (9:11, 17). According to the text, Paul regained his sight, was baptized, ate food, and was strengthened. Nothing would indicate a need to leave the house, and of course this passage does not mention any water. It is highly improbable that after he regained his sight Paul's baptism was done with immersion, but a sprinkling of Paul would fit all that was customary for the Jewish Christians. The immersion would not be likely since Scripture does not reveal any indoor bathtubs in Paul's day and, even so, what we do know about their baths was that they poured water over themselves as opposed to being immersed (Lev. 15:13).

The Symbolical Application for the Blood of Christ Requires a Sprinkling Mode

While studying the origin of biblical baptism in the Old Testament, we discover the necessity of being sprinkled by blood for the forgiveness of our sins. In the New Testament, we are told Christ's bloody sacrifice was a once-for-all sufficient sacrifice (Heb. 10:10-18). Christ never again needs to spill his blood for us. Now the blood we need for our atonement is spiritually applied.

It is interesting that the symbol used in the New Testament to describe the application of the blood of Christ is sprinkling.

> For if the blood of goats and bulls and the ashes of a heifer sprinkling those who have been defiled sanctify for the cleansing of the flesh, how much more will the blood of Christ, who through the eternal Spirit offered Himself without blemish to God, cleanse your conscience from dead works to serve the living God?
>
> —Heb. 9:13-14

> Let us draw near with a sincere heart in full assurance of faith, having our hearts sprinkled clean from an evil conscience and our bodies washed with pure water.
>
> —Heb. 10:22

> And to Jesus, the mediator of a new covenant, and to the sprinkled blood, which speaks better than the blood of Abel.
>
> —Heb. 12:24

> According to the foreknowledge of God the Father, by the sanctifying work of the Spirit, to obey Jesus Christ and be sprinkled with His blood: May grace and peace be yours in the fullest measure.
>
> —1 Pet. 1:2

It would be quite unusual to perform the sacrament of baptism using a mode that was different from that used for the application of Christ's blood, namely sprinkling. First Peter 1:2 makes it clear that those who are chosen by God for salvation were chosen so that they could "obey Jesus Christ and be *sprinkled* with His blood." This spiritual sprinkling must take place on all who are in Christ. Does this mean all believers are to be baptized by sprinkling in Christ? Being commanded to be sprinkled with Christ's blood may seem strange to someone not living in Peter's day. Sprinkling blood was a primary aspect of the worship of God for the Israelites until the time of Christ. How are we to obey the command to be sprinkled with the blood of Christ? God's Word reveals three occasions for the sprinkling of blood:

> First, for cleansing: When someone was cleansed from their sin.
>
> —Lev. 14:1-7; Heb. 9:10, 13, 14, 19-23; Num. 19:9

> Second, for covenant community inclusion: When someone was included in God's covenant community—after the people had promised to be God's faithful people they were then sprinkled with the blood of the covenant.
>
> —Exod. 24:1-8

> Third, for calling: When someone was set apart for the service of God (Exod. 29:20-22; Lev. 8:30). The priests of the tabernacle were sprinkled with the blood of the sacrificial lamb when they were sanctified for priestly service.

God wanted his people under the old covenant to be sprinkled with the blood of lambs, cows, and rams to show their cleansing from sin. And he wanted it to show their union to the covenant community and their appointment to the service of God. In the same way, God wants his people who are under the new covenant sealed by the blood of Christ to be sprinkled in this once and for all sacrifice of Christ, a sacrifice uniting us to the new covenant community, cleansing us from sin, and appointing us into his service.

The sprinkling of the blood in the Old Testament was an outward sign of an inward reality. The sprinkling of blood was symbolic of being cleansed from sin, included in God's covenant, and set apart for his service. The sprinkling of the old covenant is now commanded to be carried on as a sprinkling in the new covenant. The only difference is that the old bloody sprinklings are now performed with water since the blood of Christ once and for all fulfills the need for a blood sacrifice. Hebrews 9:10 calls the Old Testament sprinklings baptisms. All three categories of Old Testament sprinklings/baptisms can be seen in the Hebrews 9:9-28 passage. Baptism into Christ symbolizes our cleansing from sin (9:12-14, 22), our being set apart for his ministry (9:14, "to serve"), and our inclusion into God's covenant people (9:15-22, we enter the "new covenant").

In 1 Peter 1:2 we are commanded to "obey Jesus Christ and be sprinkled with His blood." This sprinkling implies more than an imaginary act we are to make in our minds in reference to Christ. If sprinkling in the New Testament is not the same as in the Old Testament, how else can we keep the command in 1 Peter? The sprinkling of the blood of Christ is now seen through the water of baptism and it shows forth what God wants to see. He wants to see us covenantally united to him and his people, cleansed from sin, and appointed to his service.

Discussion and Study Questions

1. What are the differences between the etymological and exegetical approach to discerning the biblical mode of baptism? When would the use of etymology be appropriate in biblical interpretation?
2. John the Baptist was the last Old Testament prophet and priest, the forerunner of Christ, the one who set the stage for a baptism

into Christ as part of the new covenant. Describe the kind of baptism John would need to employ to fully satisfy the Pharisees who show up to examine him in the gospel of John.

3. How does John 3:25-26 reinforce the understanding that John's baptism had to be by sprinkling or pouring?
4. Explain how Christ completes and fulfills the ceremonial ritual sprinklings of the Old Testament. Does God anywhere command his people to abandon his symbol of sprinkling in favor of a new symbol of immersing? If so, why does the apostle Peter proclaim that we were chosen to be sprinkled with the blood of Jesus Christ (1 Pet. 1:2)?
5. Over two hundred times the words *sprinkling* and *pouring* are found in the Bible, but the words *immerse, immersion,* or *immersing* are never found. What does that tell us about a God who is known for his clarity of revelation to believers? With the clear pattern of sprinkling and pouring in the worship of the people of God, could those living in the Old Testament era or those living at the time of Christ imagine "going to church" and not seeing some form of sprinkling or pouring? Would it be rather odd for God to desire his New Testament believers to begin a practice of immersing without some explanation as to why he was changing his long established symbolism for cleansing and union with God?
6. Have you been taught that the word *baptism* only means immersion? How does that square with God's use of the term? What would be the ramifications of needing to discover the use of God's words outside of the Bible?
7. God has plainly given us the mission to baptize his people in every ethnic group in the world (Matt. 28:19). How do we obey this command if we assume a mode of baptism that is dysfunctional in some places and with some people? Would God command what we cannot by his grace perform?
8. Some say, "Baptism by immersion best pictures the cleansing from sin through the work of Christ (Titus 3:5-6)." Notice how

the Titus reference has the words "He poured out." Why do we believe we can choose what we believe "best pictures the cleansing from sin through the work of Christ," rather than pull from God's word his long-term symbol for this picture? It would be quite unusual to perform the sacrament of baptism using a mode that was different from that used for the application of Christ's blood, namely sprinkling (1 Pet. 1:2).

9. What is the three-fold reason God has appointed "sprinklings" for his people? How can each of these reasons be seen in our present-day baptism services?

Chapter 4

Removing Obstructions to the Beauty and Benefits of Baptism

HAVE YOU EVER met a person who has studied the more than ninety pertinent references to sprinkling and pouring in the Bible who still believes there is biblical evidence for immersion? Have you ever met someone who considered the various baptisms mentioned in Hebrews chapter nine performed by sprinkling, and considered the prophecy sections of Scripture pointing forward to a time of sprinkling with the Messiah and the new covenant, and yet still believes there is biblical evidence for immersion? Such people surely exist, and when you ask them what more they need to be convinced of baptism by sprinkling, they express things they cannot see past—obstructions. When looking over a wall across the countryside, sometimes we can only see the mountaintops. The view is so obstructed that none of the beautiful valleys and plains and rivers between the mountaintops can be seen. It is possible to become comfortable with a disconnected and disjointed landscape when that is all that is seen. The missing parts are not noticed. But there is more beauty than can be imagined when the obstruction is removed.

Let us consider a few obstructions that need to be removed before baptism by sprinkling or pouring can be fully embraced.

Help with Seeing the "Out of Water" Passages Correctly

Matthew 3:16 states that "Jesus came up immediately from the water." Some read this text and can't see past a picture of immersion. If Jesus went down into the water, and then came up from the water, how could anything but immersion describe what took place? But this is a mental obstruction that will not be removed until we realize that God does not give us this language to teach us the proper mode of baptism. The text simply does not tell us how much water is used in the baptism—that is just not the way the text is specifically constructed. We cannot discern from this verse whether Jesus and John the Baptist went into the water just far enough to sprinkle and pour, or far enough to be completely submerged—the text simply does not reveal this information.

If the text is not designed to teach us the mode of baptism, then why does God give it to us? This is a good question, since it leads us to an interpretation that fits the context. Notice God's emphasis in this passage on the sequence of events in Christ's ministry. The full text reads, "*After* being baptized, Jesus came up *immediately* from the water; *and behold*, the heavens were opened, *and he saw* the Spirit of God descending as a dove *and behold*, a voice out of the heavens said, "This is My beloved Son, in whom I am well-pleased" (3:16-17, emphases added). The passage beams with what is almost uncontainable excitement. It reads like the language of an excited messenger who has to slow down his speech so you can understand him.

The emphasis in Matthew 3:16-17 is not on coming up from the water, but on what happens immediately after that. Or, to say it a different way, the emphasis is not on coming up from the water but on what happens because of the baptism, or because righteousness was fulfilled. "But Jesus answering said to him, 'Permit it at this time; for in this way it is fitting for us to fulfill all righteousness.' Then he permitted Him" (Matt 3:15). We are told twice in 3:16-17 to stop and look closely at the significance of this thing (*and behold*). God the Father opens the heavens, sends down his Spirit in a visible presence, and then sends forth an audible voice. How often does that occur? John the Baptist understood that the significance of this event was to recognize Jesus as the one who takes away the sin of his people:

> "I did not recognize Him, but so that He might be manifested to Israel, I came baptizing in water." John testified saying, "I have seen the Spirit descending as a dove out of heaven, and He remained upon Him. I did not recognize Him, but He who sent me to baptize in water said to me, 'He upon whom you see the Spirit descending and remaining upon Him, this is the One who baptizes in the Holy Spirit.' I myself have seen, and have testified that this is the Son of God." Again the next day John was standing with two of his disciples, and he looked at Jesus as He walked, and said, "Behold, the Lamb of God!"
>
> —John 1:31-36

God does not want us to miss his love for and approval of his Son, who is now entering into his high priestly role of taking away the sins of his people. The baptism of Christ marked the last thing that needed to happen before the Lord could begin his earthly ministry as our redeemer. God does not want us to miss Christ's righteousness fulfilled or his priestly work begun, and so he opens the heavens to speak directly. That is the emphasis in Matthew 3:15-17—not the mode of baptism, but the rich beauty of God the Father's passion for his Son to love us to the point of death on a cross. He literally screams from heaven, "Stop! Look at my beloved Son. I am so proud of what he is doing, so don't miss the significance of all this!"

There is no dearth of people who try proving immersion from phrases like "went down into the water" and "came up from the water." When I hear them, I think about the time my children were learning to swim. They "went down into" and "came up out of" the water many times before I ever succeeded at getting them to wet their heads. Many times we go in and out of the water without being immersed. We must be careful not to allow our imaginations or prejudices to read into Scripture what is not there.

There is another "out of the water" passage that needs to be addressed. Some have proposed that Acts 8:36-39 teaches immersion. The text reads this way:

> As they went along the road they came to some water; and the eunuch said, "Look! Water! What prevents me from being baptized?" And Philip said, "If you believe with all your heart, you may." And he answered and said, "I believe that Jesus Christ is the Son of God." And he ordered the chariot to stop; and they both went down into the water, Philip as well as the eunuch, and he baptized him. When they came up out of the water, the Spirit of the Lord snatched Philip away; and the eunuch no longer saw him, but went on his way rejoicing.

But when this text is used for this purpose, usually the words *they* and *both* are ignored: "And *they both* went down into the water, Philip as well as the eunuch; and he baptized him. And when *they* came up out of the water..." (emphasis added). The phrases "went down into" and "came up out of" describe an action performed by both Philip and the eunuch. Surely no one would claim that Philip immersed himself on this occasion. If then these phrases do not teach Philip's immersion, how can they be used to prove the eunuch's immersion? This passage most certainly lets us know that both Philip and the eunuch were *at* the water, *near* the water, and *in* the water, but nothing says they were *under* the water. The phrases "went down" and "came up" are here to reveal something they both did, like get down from their chariot and then return to it. Only *one* was baptized, and that was the eunuch.

It should be granted that just because Philip and the eunuch were in the desert is not proof that there was insufficient water for an immersion. It might be improbable that the terms of this text could support the presence of a well or pool or stream deep enough for an immersion, but it is not impossible. There may have indeed been enough water for an immersion, but that does not mean an immersion occurred. As a matter of fact, the context certainly leads us away from this interpretation. As Philip and the eunuch traveled, they came upon some water and the eunuch said, "Look! Water!"

(8:36). The language indicates either his surprise to see water in the desert (meaning there wasn't likely a river or much water in that desert), or his surprise to see the opportunity to fulfill what he had been reading about and what Philip had been explaining to him from the Scriptures. Let us suppose the second of these options and that the eunuch would not have been surprised to see sufficient water. The text reveals the eunuch was reading Isaiah 53, and that Philip began from Isaiah explaining to him things about Christ:

> Now the passage of Scripture which he was reading was this: "He was led as a sheep to slaughter; and as a lamb before its shearer is silent, so he does not open his mouth. In humiliation His judgment was taken away; who will relate His generation? For His life is removed from the earth." The eunuch answered Philip and said, "Please tell me, of whom does the prophet say this? Of himself or of someone else?" Then Philip opened his mouth, and beginning from this Scripture he preached Jesus to him."
>
> —Acts 8:32-35

In that day, there were no Bibles separated into chapters and verses. Isaiah was normally read from one of two scrolls (the book was divided into two scrolls because it was so long). If Philip was reading what we call the fifty-second and fifty-third chapters of the book of Isaiah, then he was reading about the coming of Jesus as the one who would "sprinkle many nations" (Isa. 52:15). This verse is only seven verses away from Isaiah 53:7, the passage which Acts 8:32 tells us the eunuch was reading when Philip came up into the chariot to teach him. How wonderfully surprising that the eunuch could have the application of the Scripture being explained to him by the apostle Philip! No wonder he said, "Look! Water!" This was exciting, for now he could receive Christ and have the sign of being "sprinkled with his blood"—baptism (1 Pet.1:2). The Scriptures came alive for him under the presence and power of the Holy Spirit. It is impossible to squeeze the concept of immersion out of these passages in Isaiah where Philip spoke to the eunuch.

Since neither the Matthew 3:16 nor the Acts 8:36-39 passages teach immersion without misinterpretation of the verses in their context, we need to let our "out of water" obstruction fall away. Beyond this, we need to also gently direct those who still can't see the beauty of these passages of Scripture to keep their interpretation within its context. Let us pray that we all may see more clearly the glory of Christ and the consistency of his word in these areas.

Help with Seeing the Baptism of Christ Correctly

> Then Jesus arrived from Galilee at the Jordan coming to John, to be baptized by him. But John tried to prevent Him, saying, "I have need to be baptized by You, and do You come to me?" But Jesus answering said to him, "Permit it at this time; for in this way it is fitting for us to fulfill all righteousness." Then he permitted Him. After being baptized, Jesus came up immediately from the water; and behold, the heavens were opened, and he saw the Spirit of God descending as a dove and lighting on Him, and behold, a voice out of the heavens said, "This is My beloved Son, in whom I am well-pleased."
>
> —Matt. 3:13-17

Here we see that Christ was baptized by John but that he did not receive the "baptism of John." The baptism of John was for sinners and represented repentance for the forgiveness of sins (Matt. 3:11). Jesus was not a sinner and therefore could not repent or receive forgiveness for sins. John's baptism was also to prepare people for receiving Christ. Christ did not need preparation for receiving himself. Therefore, though Jesus' baptism was by John, it was a different baptism than John administered to others at the Jordan River.

The fact that John was initially unwilling to baptize Jesus indicates that he considered it improper to class Jesus with the others who were coming to him for baptism. John only changed his mind on this because Jesus said it would "fulfill all righteousness" for him to be baptized. (Deuteronomy 6:25 says, "It will be righteousness for us if we are careful to observe all this commandment before the Lord our God, just as He commanded us.") Jesus was saying that he had to be baptized to fulfill Old Testament law. What law?

> Again the Lord spoke to Moses, saying, "Take the Levites from among the sons of Israel and cleanse them." Thus you shall do to them, for their cleansing: *sprinkle* purifying water on them, and let them use a razor over their whole body and wash their clothes, and they will be clean.
>
> —Num. 8:5-7, emphasis added

The law Christ was fulfilling is found in this Numbers passage, and the "cleansing" and "sprinkling" in this passage is what the writer of Hebrews calls one of the "various washings" or "various baptisms" of the Old Testament (Heb. 9:10). Being anointed by sprinkling was part of the ceremony for the ordination to priesthood. Christ was and is a priest (Heb. 3:1; 4:14; 5:5; 9:11). His baptism by John was the ceremonial act of his ordination to priesthood. Christ's baptism was by sprinkling as an anointing. God refers to Christ's anointing by the Holy Spirit (Acts 10:38) and the Holy Spirit came down at his baptism. Christ was baptized with water by John the Baptist and with the Holy Spirit by God. In neither case is there any mention of immersion, or any need for it.

Before a man could be priest, he was first required to be thirty years old (Num. 4:3, 47). Christ's age is specifically mentioned as being thirty years old in Luke 3:23. Second, he had to be called of God (1 Chron. 23:13; Exod. 28:1). Christ was called of God (Heb. 5:4-10); he did not thrust himself into the office of High Priest. Third, he had to be sprinkled with water (Num. 8:6-7). Christ was anointed by being sprinkled with water by John the Baptist (Matt. 3:13-17). He did not have to be shaved or washed, as did other priests, since these things dealt with removing sins, and Christ had no sin.

The Levities were given to priestly work. Christ was sprinkled like a Levite to be set aside for priestly service, not only for Jews (of Aaronic order) but for the whole world, according to the order of Melchizedek (Heb. 5:4-10). Christ was set aside by one who was already a priest, namely, John the Baptist. This was an Old Testament stipulation (Exod. 29:9; Num. 25:13). John was a priest by inheritance (Luke 1:5, 13). Christ came to John "to fulfill all righteousness," to meet the last and final demand of the law for Old Testament priests before they could begin public ministry. He had already been called of God and had grown to thirty years of age. Christ came to fulfill it all. Being sprinkled by John the Baptist was crucial for Christ's obedience to the law and installation into priestly ministry. Being immersed would have been contrary to the law and would have failed to usher in Christ's priestly ministry, as the context so clearly indicates.

Some may have a hard time calling Christ's baptism an anointing when the Bible called it a baptism. But we must understand the word baptism can be understood as an anointing by sprinkling, which Christ himself reveals for us in Mark 11:15-33:

> Then they came to Jerusalem. And He entered the temple and began to drive out those who were buying and selling in the temple, and overturned the tables of the money changers and the seats of those who were selling doves; and He would not permit anyone to carry merchandise through the temple. And He began to teach and say to them, "Is it not written, 'MY HOUSE SHALL BE CALLED A HOUSE OF PRAYER FOR ALL THE NATIONS'? But you have made it a ROBBERS' DEN." The chief priests and the scribes heard this, and began seeking how to destroy Him; for they were afraid of Him, for the whole crowd was astonished at His teaching. When evening came, they would go out of the city. As they were passing by in the morning, they saw the fig tree withered from the roots up. Being reminded, Peter said to Him, "Rabbi, look, the fig tree which You cursed has withered." And Jesus answered saying to them, "Have faith in God. Truly I say to you, whoever says to this mountain, 'Be taken up and cast into the sea,' and does not doubt in his heart, but believes that what he says is going to happen, it will be granted him. Therefore I say to you, all things for which you pray and ask, believe that you have received them, and they will be granted you. Whenever you stand praying, forgive, if you have anything against anyone,

> so that your Father who is in heaven will also forgive you your transgressions. [But if you do not forgive, neither will your Father who is in heaven forgive your transgressions."] They came again to Jerusalem. And as He was walking in the temple, the chief priests and the scribes and the elders came to Him, and began saying to Him, "By what authority are You doing these things, or who gave You this authority to do these things?" And Jesus said to them, "I will ask you one question, and you answer Me, and then I will tell you by what authority I do these things. "Was the baptism of John from heaven, or from men? Answer Me." They began reasoning among themselves, saying, "If we say, 'From heaven,' He will say, 'then why did you not believe him?' But shall we say, 'From men'?"—they were afraid of the people, for everyone considered John to have been a real prophet. Answering Jesus, they said, "We do not know." And Jesus said to them, "Nor will I tell you by what authority I do these things."

This account of Jesus' cleansing the temple reveals Christ's own explanation of his baptism being none other than his priestly anointing. Only a priest would have authority to cleanse the temple, and Christ directs us to see that he was a priest who received priestly authority according to Old Testament law when he was baptized by John. Thus, John's baptism was for Jesus an anointing. Since he had been ordained a priest at his baptism, he had authority to cleanse the temple.

It is interesting to note in this passage that the high priest, scribes, and elders did not bring up their problem with what Christ had done (cleanse the temple), but only with where he had received his authority. Cleansing the temple was under the authority of the priests. Where had Christ gotten such authority? In answer to this question, Jesus brings up the baptism of John. If they acknowledge that John was a God-called, God-ordained priest, then by default they must acknowledge that Jesus had authority to cleanse the temple since Jesus was anointed a priest by John.

Could Christ's anointing by John the Baptist be symbolized by immersion? The answer is no. Anointing, by biblical definition, was performed by sprinkling to fulfill God's specific law. We cannot change the obedience required by God's law. If Jesus was immersed and not sprinkled with water, he was not the "Christ" or the "Messiah," for both terms mean "Anointed One." Anointing was by sprinkling or pouring. If you take away Jesus' anointing by sprinkling at the baptism by John and call it an immersion, then where else was Jesus anointed? He had to be anointed to be our Savior. The only place God records his anointing as a priest was at the baptism by John.

If Jesus was immersed at his baptism, then he did not "fulfill all righteousness." There is an Old Testament requirement for his sprinkling which he must complete to "fulfill all righteousness." There is no Old Testament requirement for his immersion. Whether immersing Christ took place or not would not matter. But his sprinkling was an absolute necessity for his sinless perfection. Those who speak of Christ as being immersed by John rob him of being both the Messiah and the sinless one—unless they prove that he was also at some point sprinkled.

Help for Seeing Baptism by Sprinkling as Fulfilled Prophecy

In addition to fulfilling every law, the Lord also came to fulfill prophecy. It was prophesied that he would be born of a virgin (Isa. 7:14) and he was (Matt. 1:23); that he should be born in Bethlehem (Mic. 5:2) and called out of Egypt (Hosea 11:1) and he was (Matt. 2:15). Another prophecy was that "he would sprinkle many nations" (Isa. 52:15) and he did (John 3:25-26). Since there is no prophecy demanding immersion, to employ that mode for baptizing is to create an obstruction to the beauty and benefits of baptism.

Consider the beauty of Ezekiel's prophecy finding partial fulfillment in the book of Acts. This beauty is likely to be missed until we see sprinkling as the right mode for baptism.

The Prophecy of Ezekiel	→	The Acts Fulfillment
For I will take you from the nations, gather you from all the lands and bring you into your own land. *Ezekiel 36:24*	→	Now there were Jews living in Jerusalem, devout men from every nation under heaven. *Acts 2:5*
Then I will sprinkle clean water on you, and you will be clean; I will cleanse you from all your filthiness and from all your idols. *Ezekiel 36:25*	→	So then, those who had received his word were baptized; and that day there were added about three thousand souls. *Acts 2:41*
Moreover, I will give you a new heart and put a new spirit within you; and I will remove the heart of stone from your flesh and give you a heart of flesh. *Ezekiel 36:26*	→	Day by day continuing with one mind in the temple, and breaking bread from house to house, they were taking their meals together with gladness and sincerity of heart. *Acts 2:46*
I will put My Spirit within you and cause you to walk in My statutes, and you will be careful to observe My ordinances. *Ezekiel 36:27*	→	And when they had prayed, the place where they had gathered together was shaken, and they were all filled with the Holy Spirit and *began* to speak the word of God with boldness. *Acts 4:31*

Proposing immersion as the mode of baptism at Pentecost adds to the Word of God and ignores God's prophecy. With sprinkling as the mode for baptism, the prophecy and its fulfillment are like a seamless garment.

Help for Seeing Baptism by Sprinkling as Holy Spirit Symbolism

Baptism has often been presented as something we do to present ourselves to the church as those who have made personal decisions for Christ. Let us move beyond this ceremony to the reality of spiritual baptism, something God does through the person and work of the Holy Spirit. To be clear, I am speaking of two different baptisms: There is the ceremonial baptism, which is the ritual, and there is the spiritual union and conversion to Christ, which is the real baptism. The ritual baptism is that which symbolizes the work of the Holy Spirit, and the real baptism is the wonderful work of the Holy Spirit in the inner person. Never does the New Testament picture the believer in Christ being dipped into the Holy Spirit or submerged under the Holy Spirit. Rather, the Holy Spirit always comes upon the believer rather than the believer coming upon the Spirit. When this is understood, our baptism ceremonies cease to be human-centered celebrations of our obedience in turning to Christ and become God-centered celebrations of God's free grace coming to us.

With the coming of Christ's ministry, we were promised a baptism with the Holy Spirit and with fire (Matt. 3:11; Mark 1:8). The Holy Spirit baptism came at Pentecost. Jesus said, "John baptized with water, but you will be baptized with the Holy Spirit not many days from now" (Acts 1:5). Jesus has expressly said the coming of the Holy Spirit upon the disciples at Pentecost was the baptism of the Holy Spirit and fire. The way the Holy Spirit and fire came upon the disciples is quite contrary to any idea of immersion. No reasonable argument can be understood from this text that the disciples were immersed into the Holy Spirit or fire, not even in a figurative way. The Holy Spirit is represented as something that has come down upon the disciples (Acts 1:8), and the fire "rested on each one of them" (Acts 2:3). The promises here fulfilled were that the Holy Spirit would be poured out, shed forth, and sprinkled (Isa. 32:15; Joel 2:28; Prov. 1:23; Ezek. 36:25-27). This language in no way leads us to assume a need for immersion.

Notice the inseparable link between the *ritual* water baptism and the *real* Holy Spirit baptism. Consider the following:

> As for me, I baptize you with water for repentance, but He who is coming after me is mightier than I, and I am not fit to remove His sandals; He will baptize you with the Holy Spirit and fire.
> —Matt. 3:11

> John answered and said to them all, "As for me, I baptize you with water; but One is coming who is mightier than I, and I am

> not fit to untie the thong of His sandals; He will baptize you with the Holy Spirit and fire."
>
> —Luke 3:16

> And as I began to speak, the Holy Spirit fell upon them just as He did upon us at the beginning. And I remembered the word of the Lord, how He used to say, "John baptized with water, but you will be baptized with the Holy Spirit."
>
> —Acts 11:15-16

The ritual has no purpose if it does not symbolize the real. Since the ritual is to symbolize the baptism of the Holy Spirit, it cannot be administered by immersion, since the manner in which the Holy Spirit comes upon us is never described in immersionist terminology. Rather, the Holy Spirit is poured out upon us, or falls out upon us. These verses do not necessarily prove sprinkling as the mode for ceremonial baptism, but they do show sprinkling to be a consistent symbol for spiritual baptism.

The Bible does not say ritual baptism is to symbolize death, burial, and resurrection. The Bible clearly indicates that it is Holy Spirit baptism that is to be depicted by the symbol of water poured out or sprinkled out. In other words, the external symbol must appropriately symbolize the internal reality. Only sprinkling or pouring does this.

What, then, is the right mode of baptism? Since baptism means union with God in Christ through the Holy Spirit, the best symbol of this is by pouring or sprinkling with water. No saving or sanctifying operations of the Holy Spirit are pictured by immersion. The pouring or sprinkling also symbolizes the basis for this union, namely, cleansing from our sin through the sacrificial work of Christ. Whether speaking about a ceremonial baptism or a spiritual baptism, the Scripture, both Old and New Testaments, consistently instruct us to baptize by sprinkling. Never have we read in the Scripture that God will "immerse us in his Spirit" or "put us all the way under clean water" or "plunge us underneath his Spirit."

Since New Testament baptism is to signify the Holy Spirit uniting himself to us and applying all the work of Christ to our account, let us observe how consistently this is represented by every revelation of God on this subject—all can be visibly pictured with either pouring or sprinkling. Should there not be a simple and clear consistency between the ritual baptism and the real Holy Spirit baptism when the baptism water is applied?

> For I will pour out water on the thirsty land and streams on the dry ground; I will pour out My Spirit on your offspring and My blessing on your descendants.
>
> —Isa. 44:3

> Then I will sprinkle clean water on you, and you will be clean; I will cleanse you from all your filthiness and from all your idols. Moreover, I will give you a new heart and put a new spirit within you; and I will remove the heart of stone from your flesh and give you a heart of flesh. I will put My Spirit within you and cause you to walk in My statutes, and you will be careful to observe My ordinances.
>
> —Ezek. 36:25-27

> Sow with a view to righteousness, Reap in accordance with kindness; Break up your fallow ground, For it is time to seek the Lord until He comes to rain righteousness on you.
>
> —Hosea 10:12

> I will be like the dew to Israel; He will blossom like the lily, and he will take root like the cedars of Lebanon.
>
> —Hosea 14:5

> It will come about after this that I will pour out My Spirit on all mankind; and your sons and daughters will prophesy, Your old men will dream dreams, Your young men will see visions. Even on the male and female servants I will pour out My Spirit in those days.
>
> —Joel 2:28-29

"And behold, I am sending forth the promise of My Father upon you; but you are to stay in the city until you are clothed with power from on high."

—Luke 24:49

John testified saying, "I have seen the Spirit descending as a dove out of heaven, and He remained upon Him.

—John 1:32

But you will receive power when the Holy Spirit has come upon you; and you shall be My witnesses both in Jerusalem, and in all Judea and Samaria, and even to the remotest part of the earth.

—Acts 1:8

"And it shall be in the last days," God says, "that I will pour forth of My spirit on all mankind; and your sons and your daughters shall prophesy, and your young men shall see visions, and your old men shall dream dreams."

—Acts 2:17

Therefore having been exalted to the right hand of God, and having received from the Father the promise of the Holy Spirit, He has poured forth this which you both see and hear.

—Acts 2:33

While Peter was still speaking these words, the Holy Spirit fell upon all those who were listening to the message.

—Acts 10:44

And as I began to speak, the Holy Spirit fell upon them just as He did upon us at the beginning.

—Acts 11:15

How does God our Father baptize with the Holy Spirit? He plainly reveals that when he baptizes with the Holy Spirit, he does so by bringing the Holy Spirit down upon us and never by putting us into him. Since our water baptism is to reflect this work of the Holy Spirit coming to us, why would we want to assume a mode of administration like immersion when it creates an obvious visual disconnection from what God is communicating and doing? Baptism does not mean to sprinkle or pour; it means a union with God through Christ and the Holy Spirit. The picture God gives us through the Holy Spirit of how this union occurs is his coming down from above to rest upon us. The mode he frequently uses throughout his Word to communicate this action is that of sprinkling and pouring.

Part of the picture in baptism is that of being cleansed from sin through the sprinkling of the blood of Jesus (Acts 2:38; 22:16; 1 Cor. 6:11; 1 Pet. 3:21) by the work of the Holy Spirit (Titus 3:5; John 3:5; Col. 2:11). It is the Holy Spirit who makes baptism effective, thus making it fitting for the mode used in baptism to picture the Holy Spirit coming down from heaven to us.

Help in Seeing No Problem with Time

After Peter's sermon in the second chapter of Acts, about three thousand souls were added to the church through baptism (Acts 2:41). Let's assume Peter finished preaching by 10:00 AM, and there were still eight hours left in the day for baptizing. If this were the case, each of the twelve apostles would have to baptize two hundred-fifty persons each—more than thirty-one persons each hour, or a little better than one person every two minutes, nonstop for eight hours.

Though this could be done, enormous organization, perseverance, and commitment from all participants to a speedy entrance in and out of the water would have had to take place. It seems unlikely. If there was not a full day available for baptizing, or if any of the apostles could not stand that long, or needed to take a bathroom break (or any number of other things), the improbability becomes even greater. If you baptize the nations by sprinkling—dipping a hyssop branch into the water and shaking it upon the people, three thousand can be baptized rather quickly. As a matter of fact, when the covenant was renewed under Moses, he sprinkled several hundred thousand people in one day using this method: "Moses took half of the blood and put it in basins, and the other half of the blood he sprinkled on the altar. Then he took the book of the covenant and read it in the hearing of the people; and they said, 'All that the Lord has spoken we will do, and we will be obedient!' So Moses took the blood and sprinkled it on the people, and said, 'Behold the blood of the covenant, which the Lord has made with you in accordance with all these words'" (Exod. 24:6-8).

Help in Seeing No Problem with Place

Was there really a place for the immersion of three thousand souls just outside Jerusalem on the day of Pentecost? Did the women robe and disrobe for the baptism, or were they prepared to wear what they had on dripping wet through Jerusalem? Was it appropriate for these women to be dipped under water by Jewish men in public? Was there a river or stream that all could easily walk in and out of without difficulty? Many believe that if the water around Jerusalem was the same as it is today, then there was only a small stream in the vicinity of Jerusalem—the brook Kedron—at the time of this baptism. And Kedron would not have been nearly sufficient for immersion. There were the public reservoirs of water (underground cisterns accessed by staircases), but it is unlikely the authorities of the city would allow three thousand people to plunge into their drinking water, especially if they were somehow related to the one they had crucified named Jesus. Such would be forbidden out of common decency, not to mention out of hatred for Jesus and his followers. Churches in our day insisting on baptizing by immersion have had many discussions in their church planting stages on where they will find sufficient water, apparel, time, and place for their baptism ceremonies. When baptisms are performed by sprinkling and pouring, as they were in the book of Acts, these discussions are unnecessary.

Help in Seeing the Problem of No Explanation

Many of our present day conflicts regarding baptism could have been handled if the apostles had taken the time to explain the order and procedure they followed to get everyone baptized on that day recorded in Acts 2. When we stop to consider all we would want them to explain, however, we find the list of questions expands if the baptism preformed was by immersion. Of first importance would be to explain what immersion means, and why they would need it. The crowd in Acts 2 was familiar with various baptisms, but they were always done in the Old Testament by sprinkling, as the writer of Hebrews has informed us (Heb. 9:10, 13, 19, 21). They were very familiar with worship services that included the priest sprinkling people, but they would not have been familiar with any immersion services or Scripture passages teaching immersion. Perhaps some of them had also seen John the Baptist in the wilderness. Jesus said, "What did you go out into the wilderness to see? A reed shaken by the wind?" (Matt. 11:7; Luke 7:24). Describing John's work in this way makes sense if he were baptizing by taking a hyssop branch and shaking it (sprinkling), especially if his baptism was primarily a message regarding cleansing from sin. King David said, "Purify me with hyssop, and I shall be clean; wash me and I shall be whiter than snow" (Ps. 51:7).

If the apostles are now to switch the past practice of baptizing by sprinkling to one of immersion, a little explanation is certainly needed. Could Peter have simply directed his audience to the burial terminology of Romans chapter six? No, Romans 6 had not yet been written. The apostle Paul had not yet begun to write Scripture since he had not yet been saved and commissioned by God. How then could three thousand people be dunked completely under water without explanation? To sprinkle them would not have been a problem. The Jews had been long awaiting the new covenant and the coming of the Messiah. They had been praying for the day when God would begin a new covenant with them and sprinkle them with clean water (Ezek. 36:24-27). They had been longing for their coming Messiah who would "sprinkle many nations" (Isa. 52:15). They had also been constantly practicing purification from their sins by sprinkling at their regular worship services.

If the apostles found themselves before a crowd of thousands who all in the same day wanted to receive the good news of cleansing from sin through union with Jesus their Messiah, if they found themselves needing to visually symbolize this gracious work and promised coming of the Holy Spirit, and if they found themselves wanting to fulfill Christ's commission to baptize disciples from every nation, all they needed to do on the day of Pentecost was to dip a branch in water and begin shaking the water on the multitude saying, "Repent and each of you be baptized in the name of Jesus Christ for the forgiveness of your sins; and you will receive the gift of the Holy Spirit. For the promise is for you and your children and for all who are far off, as many as the Lord our God will call to Himself" (Acts 2:38-39). No further explanation was needed.

DISCUSSION AND STUDY QUESTIONS

1. Why is it difficult to see that a passage including the phrase "much water" does not have to imply the use of much water in the ritual of baptism? Do any of the "much water" passages of Scripture tell us specifically how "much water" is used in the baptism service? Aside from getting into the bath tub, what are some of the times when we go "down into water" or come up "out of water" and are never immersed by the water?
2. When the eunuch of Acts 8:25-40 said, "Look! Water!" he was obviously excited. What in the Isaiah chapters fifty-two to fifty-three text was he reading that would have brought him to such a place of excitement? What insight does this Isaiah passage give us regarding the mode of baptism likely used by Philip?
3. Why would John not want to baptize Jesus? What is the essence of Jesus' explanation why John should perform a baptism for him?
4. What is meant by the phrase "to fulfill all righteousness" that Jesus uses to convince John to baptize him in Matthew 3:15? If it refers to fulfilling the law of God, then what law from God did Jesus need to keep that would have to do with him being baptized by either immersion or sprinkling?

5. What is the authority issue in question in Mark 11:15-33, and how does Jesus prove he has the authority required by all the chief priests and scribes?
6. Since Ezekiel 36 prophesied that the Holy Spirit would be poured out in the new covenant age upon God's people, and that God would at that time sprinkle clean water upon his people, how does introducing baptism by immersion on the day of this prophecy's fulfillment (Acts 2) make sense?
7. Where does God describe a baptism service as a celebration of someone's personal decision for Christ? If God does not do this, then how does he describe the celebration in a baptism service? In other words, how does the external symbolism required in a baptism service depict and enable us to celebrate the internal reality of God's grace to us through union with Christ?
8. What was the sign of the covenant used for several hundred thousand people during the time of Moses (Exod. 24:6-8)? How might this be a better picture of how the disciples were able to baptize three thousand souls in one day?
9. What would be the obstacles involved in baptizing three thousand souls on the day of Pentecost by the method of immersion? Why does God not mention any of these obstacles in the book of Acts?

Chapter 5

The Beauty and Benefits of Baptism Extended to Children

WHO SHOULD RECEIVE baptism according to Christ's direction to "Go therefore and make disciples of all the nations, baptizing them in the name of the Father and the Son and the Holy Spirit" (Matt. 28:19)? Those who receive baptism are the disciples of Jesus Christ. Yet there is more to this question, for both the Old and New Testament give instruction and examples of baptism extending beyond those who are known as Christ's disciples. Baptism should be administered to all who profess faith in Christ—along with their children. That is, both believers and believers' children are to be marked out as members of God's covenant community by baptism.

The idea of baptism extending to the children of believers may seem like a strange statement to many in a present day culture so strongly influenced by the philosophy of individualism. We are told that a person's actions are his own, not affecting those around him. But this is just not true. Let a husband and father commit adultery and it will affect his wife and children for the rest of their lives. In the same way, his godly acts are a benefit to them. God has designed a "family dynamic" into his image bearers. What we do and what happens to us has implications for our whole family.

Suppose the good news of Christ was proclaimed to an adult male who did not grow up in the church and who had never heard about Jesus Christ (an occasion we find throughout much of the New Testament). If he responds through repentance and faith to Christ and has a wife and four children, what are the implications of his salvation on his family? An investigation of this real-life scenario in Scripture reveals God's "family dynamic" through family baptism. There are several New Testament references to believers and their whole household being baptized:

> A woman named Lydia, from the city of Thyatira, a seller of purple fabrics, a worshiper of God, was listening; and the Lord opened her heart to respond to the things spoken by Paul. And when *she and her household* had been baptized, she urged us, saying, "If you have judged me to be faithful to the Lord, come into my house and stay." And she prevailed upon us.
>
> —Acts 16:14-15, emphasis added

> They said, "Believe in the Lord Jesus, and you will be saved, *you and your household.*" And they spoke the word of the Lord to him together with all who were in his house. And he took them that very hour of the night and washed their wounds, and immediately he was baptized, he and *all his household.*
>
> —Acts 16:31-33, emphasis added

> Crispus, the leader of the synagogue, believed in the Lord *with all his household*, and many of the Corinthians when they heard were believing and being baptized.
>
> —Acts 18:8, emphasis added

> Now I did baptize also *the household of Stephanas*; beyond that, I do not know whether I baptized any other.
>
> —1 Cor. 1:16, emphasis added

Why should household baptisms seem strange if baptism is a sign of God's covenantal union and love to us? If God has purchased us with the blood of his own Son, does he not own all that is ours, including our children? Would it not seem right for God to want all of his people, all he has claimed ownership over by covenant, to bear the covenant sign?

Family Baptism Issues

Some have argued that household baptisms in Scripture prove nothing. Yet we would all agree that God has some reason for revealing them to us. Some assume that God's revelation of the early church only reveals adult baptisms which occur *after* conversion. That assumption is not correct because Simon was clearly baptized *prior* to genuine conversion, that is, prior to saving faith (Acts 8:9-24). Yet let us not assume when conversion must occur until we have studied this issue with children. Let us consider the household baptisms and the probability of them including children.

First of all, have not the children of covenant-keeping families throughout Scripture been treated differently than the children of pagan families? Why would we think God would want to treat the children of the church the same as those in the pagan society? Is there a biblical command that bids us to exclude children from the covenant blessings of God that they enjoyed in the Old Testament? Let us look at the early church baptisms with covenant eyes for all covenant members. If covenant blessings are only for adults, then so be it, but if they are also for children, then let us not exclude them.

Adult Baptisms (no household present)	**Family (whole household) Baptisms**
At Pentecost—Acts 2:41 (probably all men, 2:5, 42, but maybe also some women, 1:14. Total about three thousand)	Cornelius and his family—Acts 10:22-48; 11:14
In Samaria—Acts 8:12-13 (both men and women, and even Simon, an unregenerate)	Lydia and her family—Acts 16:14-15
Ethiopian eunuch—Acts 8:25-40	Philippian jailer and his family—Acts 16:31-34
Saul—Acts 9:1-19	Crispus and his family—Acts 18:8; 1 Cor. 1:14
Disciples of John—Acts 19:1-7 (about twelve men)	Stephanas and his family—1 Cor. 1:16
Gaius—1 Cor. 1:14	

The above table presents the case studies on baptism God has given us regarding the early church. *Not once* do we see an adult being baptized in the presence of his or her family without the whole family being baptized. In other words, parents never get baptized and leave their children to grow up to be baptized whenever they desire or profess faith. The Bible does not just record baptisms of adult believers. It records whole household baptisms, and even a baptism of an adult non-believer who was a sorcerer. Of course, no one today can prove how old the household members were, but how likely would it be that any household in the first century (or any other century) would not have young children? We cannot say that household baptisms were an anomaly because they are just as frequent as adult baptisms—almost one for one in the record God gives us. Of the adult baptisms presented, two of the men (Saul and the Ethiopian eunuch) didn't have children, so they definitely couldn't have them baptized. Of the crowd at Pentecost, it would not be expected that they would have had their families with them, and yet Peter clearly assures them that their promise in baptism includes their children. "For the promise is for you and your children and for all who are far off, as many as the Lord our God will call to Himself" (Acts 2:39).

Of the remaining baptisms on record (which are primarily family baptisms), it stretches credulity to believe that the households only included adults and that every one of these adults professed faith in Christ at exactly the same time as the head of the household so they could be baptized at exactly the same time. I have never heard anyone give a testimony to this kind of thing happening in their family—God waiting to save them all as adults at exactly the same time. Perhaps the first century church were merely putting their faith in a God who included their children in his saving love and desired the sign of his covenant love on each household where he had begun his saving work (Gen. 17:7; Deut. 30:6; Ps. 103:17; Isa. 59:21; Jer. 31:36-37; Acts 2:39; 16:31; 1 Cor. 7:14). This is why Acts 2:39 does *not* read, "the promise is for you so you should be baptized, and the promise is also for your children, *but they should not be baptized.*"

One more interesting note is that the New Testament never describes the baptism of an adult born of Christian parents! It would have been unusual for those born of Christian parents to not have been baptized as children.

Infant Baptism Introduced

There is a story in the Scriptures about a time when some people were bringing children to Jesus to receive his blessing, but the disciples sought to hinder them from coming.

> And they were bringing children to Him so that He might touch them; but the disciples rebuked them. But when Jesus saw this, He was indignant and said to them, "Permit the children to come to me; do not hinder them; for the kingdom of God belongs to such as these. Truly I say to you, whoever does not receive the kingdom of God like a child will not enter it at all." And He took them in His arms and began blessing them, laying His hands on them.
>
> —Mark 10:13-16

This is the only place in the Gospels that Jesus is described as being *indignant*. Indignation is anger over injustice, and in this situation Jesus was very displeased. He was angry over the injustice being done to children. What was wrong? In verse thirteen we see the disciples were trying to keep little children from coming to Jesus. In verse sixteen Jesus gets upset over this injustice and says, "Permit the children come to me; do not hinder them." Why? Because the kingdom of God belongs to them, or more specifically, to "such as these." In other words, Jesus is saying we should not try and keep children or those such as them from coming to Christ for that which is theirs to enjoy, namely the kingdom of God. The blessing of God's rule was theirs to enjoy—if they would just be allowed to come.

We do not know why the disciples tried to keep the children from the kingdom of God. We do not know why they felt like children were so unimportant that they should be kept from the blessings of God's rule. What we do know is that there are many people in our world today who feel the same way about keeping little children from God's blessings. Some, perhaps, hinder little children from receiving the blessings of God's kingdom out of ignorance. Others strictly teach that children have no place in the kingdom of God until they are old enough to understand the gospel and make a profession of faith in Christ. But notice that the Mark 10:13-16 passage does not say the children had to be of a certain age. As a matter of fact, it gives every indication they were very young, so young they had to be brought to Jesus, not sent, and young enough to be in a very normal fashion held in Jesus' arms. The passage does not say they had to make a profession of faith before they could come and receive the blessings of the kingdom. Jesus simply said, "Permit the children to come to me; do not hinder them; for the kingdom of God belongs to such as these."

The kingdom of God includes little children even prior to their ability to make a profession of faith in Christ. To some, it is unbelievable that God will give his kingdom blessings to those who have done nothing for it. But that is the very nature of the gospel! His kingdom and the promises which undergird it are absolutely free and unmerited. God graciously gives such things even to some little children. Let us not attempt to be wiser or more holy than God and restrict the kingdom of God to those of some magical age ("age of accountability") or to only those capable of intelligent understanding faith.

How can little children today, just like those in the first century, receive the gift of God's kingdom blessings, even before a profession of faith is made by them? They can receive the blessings based on a covenant promise from God to his people:

> Peter said to them, "Repent, and each of you be baptized in the name of Jesus Christ for the forgiveness of your sins; and you will receive the gift of the Holy Spirit. For the promise is for you and your children and for all who are far off, as many as the Lord our God will call to Himself."
>
> —Acts 2:38-39

The covenant promise "for you and your children and for all who are far off, as many as the Lord our God will call to Himself" is a reference back to God's word to Abraham in Genesis 17:7-14. And it is a reference to the covenant Spirit in Isaiah 59:21, a covenant granting blessings to "your offspring ...[and] your offspring's offspring ...from now and forever."

Infant Baptism Implications

No Christian would dispute that adult believers should be baptized since they possess what the sign of baptism signifies, namely covenantal union with God. If children, however, can be baptized prior to faith and repentance, then how do we explain this covenantal union? In what sense are they united to God that would be different from not being a baptized child of a believer? Let us investigate the promise God has given to our children when we have them baptized.

> Peter said to them, "Repent, and each of you be baptized in the name of Jesus Christ for the forgiveness of your sins; and you will receive the gift of the Holy Spirit. For the promise is for you and your children and for all who are far off, as many as the Lord our God will call to Himself."
>
> —Acts 2:38-39

The reason the apostle Peter urges believers to be baptized is on the basis of the Genesis 17:7-12 Old Testament promise, a promise that includes children. It begins with, "I will establish My covenant between Me and you and your descendants after you throughout their generations for an everlasting covenant, to be God to you and to your descendants after you." God has continued in the New Testament to include children in his promise, just as he did in the Old Testament. Peter knew that when God drew men to himself and made them his covenant people, they were obligated to put on the sign of covenantal union (circumcision in the Old Testament and baptism in the New Testament). Through this covenantal sign,

God expresses his glorious promise to be our God forever. This promise has important ramifications for the whole household, for when God saves one member of any family, his intention is to grant covenantal blessings and privileges to the whole family.

Immersionists tend to ignore God's Old Testament covenantal promise since Peter's reference to a promise (Acts 2:39) refers to the giving of the Holy Spirit (Acts 2:38). Their thinking is, how could God possibly promise the Holy Spirit to those who have yet to repent and believe in Christ? First of all, we need to see that the promise of receiving the Holy Spirit does not automatically imply receiving the Holy Spirit in a regenerative sense. By comparing Acts 2:39 with Genesis 17:7-14, we see that in the covenant God promises himself to people, but the promise of salvation to people is suspended upon conditions to be fulfilled first by the parents and then by the children. The conditions are faith, repentance, holiness, and perseverance.

To explain this further, a brief study of theology is in order, specifically a study of the Holy Spirit's work in common grace. To understand how children of believers can experience a promised work of the Holy Spirit without being regenerated, let us consider three categories of common grace here listed in progressive and ascending order:

Universal Common Grace

First is universal common grace, which includes those general blessings of God which extend to all his creation. Universal common grace would include such things as sunshine, rain, food, drink, clothing, and shelter. Humans are the image-bearers of God, but these blessings are for animal and plant life as well. Examples of the Holy Spirit's common grace work to generate life and complete the creative works of God are abundant (Job 33:4; 34:14, 15; Ps. 104:24-30; Gen. 1:2; 2:7). Life as we know it in its origin, maintenance, and development depends upon the work of the Holy Spirit. Were it not for the Holy Spirit, all creation would be dead.

General Common Grace

Second is general common grace, meaning those general blessings of the Holy Spirit upon humanity (but not animals and plants) through God's general or special revelation that morally influences people to restrain their indulgence in sin, maintain social order, and promote civil righteousness, all without renewing or regenerating the human heart (Gen. 6:3; Isa. 63:10; Acts 7:51). This is a general striving of the Holy Spirit with human beings that does not lead to repentance of sin or faith in Christ. The unregenerate grieve and resist the Holy Spirit and the Spirit limits their days upon the earth. The Holy Spirit still pours out upon men and women in common fashion many graces such as artistic skill (Exod. 28:3; 31:3; 35:30-33; Neh. 9:20), intellectual insight (Job 32:8), and the ability to make decisions and understand the complexities of living. These abilities are not innate, but due to the illuminating work of the Holy Spirit.

Covenant Common Grace

Third is covenant common grace. These blessings are common to both the elect and non-elect who live together in the covenant community. The blessings include things like the preaching of the Word, the observance of the sacraments, the external call of the gospel, and the illumination and gifts of the Holy Spirit referred to in Hebrews 6:4-6. Another example of this is 1 Corinthians 7:14: "For the unbelieving husband is sanctified through his wife, and the unbelieving wife is sanctified through her believing husband; for otherwise your children are unclean, but now they are holy." It is at this level of common grace that baptized children of believing parents reap great benefit.

The Promise of Peter

This breakdown of common grace into three categories helps us to see that though there is a grace of God common to all, it is not necessarily given to all in common fashion. Some receive more or less of God's common grace. Inwardly, in the rebellious human heart, most continue to resist this grace. The electing, regenerating grace of the Holy Spirit which penetrates hearts and draws us to Christ is a grace that is irresistible and special; it is not referred to here under the heading of common grace.

Perhaps it is easy to hold on to this concept of three levels of common grace if we compare it to the degrees of nature. It is God's nature to be holy, yet the Scripture reveals that he is not just holy; he is "Holy, Holy, Holy, is the Lord of hosts" (Isa. 6:3). In other words, God is holy to the superlative degree. He is not just declared holy (*holy* as a declarative adjective), and he is not just more holy than others who are holy (*holy* as a comparative adjective), but he is only holy and uniquely holy like none other. These degrees of nature are usually described with the words *good*, *better*, and *best*. All grace from God is good, but some grace is even better. And yet other grace is the best! Thus, universal common grace is good, general common grace is better, and the covenantal common grace is best.

Just consider the benefit of education. Children who are educated in a humanistic environment are the recipients of God's general common grace. They may not know their education is dependent upon the work of the Holy Spirit to provide them a general common grace, but it is nonetheless true. As they are enabled by God, they can receive the best education known to man. But the best of man goes only so far. This education is better than no education, but it is not the best education in any sense. The best education is only reserved for those who are the recipients of covenantal common grace. A covenantal Christian school has the work of the Holy Spirit on a higher level through the influence of the Holy Spirit in the covenant Christian community. There are benefits God gives his covenant community which do not reach those apart from Christ and outside this community.

To understand the promise Peter refers to in Acts 2:38-39, remember that it is not only to us, but to "your children and for all who are far off." The reference to those who are far off means those under your authority (Gen. 17:13-14). If the promise were restricted to the giving of the Holy Spirit in regeneration, then the implication would be that the Holy Spirit was promised to your children for their certain salvation. This, however, would be contrary to John 1:13, where God clearly states we are not regenerated as a result of our parent's faith, will, or blood. God does not promise the Holy Spirit will regenerate all of our children, but he does promise them covenantal blessings through us who believe. He promises to move them to his highest level of common grace, where they will receive special treatment through the means of grace only found within the family of obedient believers. Those who have covenantal common grace have special grace promised to them. Though real, this promise of special grace is suspended until conditions of faith, repentance, holiness, and perseverance are met.

Consider 1 Corinthians 7:14 for an example of God's covenantal common grace promised to our children:

> For the unbelieving husband is sanctified through his wife, and the unbelieving wife is sanctified through her believing husband; for *otherwise your children are unclean, but now they are holy.*
>
> —emphasis added

The immersionists usually say there is no difference between the children of believers and the children of unbelievers. But God says there is a difference. He says the children who have Christian parents are *holy* because the covenant promise includes them, and the sign of that promise (namely, baptism) should be given to them.

To be *unclean* in the sense implied in 1 Corinthians 7:14 is to be outside the covenant community, unconsecrated, and set apart *from* God. Thus, according to the same verse, to be *holy* places the children of believers *within* the covenant of grace. The sacrament of infant baptism is the only New Testament sign God has given us by which our children can be marked out and distinguished as participants in the covenant of grace. God's Word clearly reveals that his gracious covenant promise is made to believers and their seed (Gen. 17:7; Luke 1:55).

Consider David's request, "Do not cast me away from Your presence and do not take Your Holy Spirit from me" (Ps. 51:11). David saw the Holy Spirit removed from Saul. He may not have feared losing his soul or the regeneration work of the Holy Spirit, but he did fear he would not be sanctified and cleansed from his sin. He wanted to be holy, and he needed the Holy Spirit for this work, just as we and our children do. What a privilege to have God's Spirit working in our lives and in our children's lives as they live in our covenant communities.

Consider the contrast between *unclean* and *holy* as found in the Scriptures in order to understand better the meaning and impact of 1 Corinthians 7:14. In Ephesians 5:5 God says, "For this you know with certainty, that no immoral or impure person …has an inheritance in the kingdom of Christ and God." This means no unclean person inherits the kingdom of God. But doesn't the kingdom belong to the children of believers? The same adjective for *unclean* found in Ephesians 5:5 is used over twenty times for demons or unclean spirits (Mark 5:12-13). The word for *holy* is used for "holy angels" (Rev. 14:10), "holy apostles and prophets" (Rev. 18:20), the "holy child Jesus" (Acts 4:27), and the "Holy Spirit" (Matt. 1:18). The word *holy* is also used over sixty times as *saints* (Col. 1:12; 1 Thess. 3:13). First Corinthians 7:14 is one of those references where *holy* points to those who are *regarded* as saints and those who are not.

Consequently, when the children of believers are baptized, they are brought under the *obligations* of the covenant. At this point, the parents and church have a solemn duty not to assume or take for granted the child's election. The child does not have the privilege of full church membership until he or she makes a credible confession of faith. We must seek their salvation through repentance and faith in Christ.

Nevertheless, there remains a great advantage for the baptized infant. The covenant child is placed in the context of the covenant community where the means of grace are applied to his or her life. Just as there was great advantage in the Old Testament for the Jew to be within God's covenant community prior to his entrance into the Promised Land (Rom. 3:1-2), so there is great advantage for the covenant child today. The covenant child receives the preaching of the Word, prayers, and fellowship of the saints as the privileged means God employs to bring his people to complete salvation in Christ. At issue is how the Lord views our children. Are they set apart and special in God's eyes? Or are they just like the children of atheists, Muslims, Buddhists, and others outside the Christian community?

Baptism is a sign of God marking us out and making us covenant members. It is God's sign of his gracious cleansing from sin by the Holy Spirit and the application of Christ's blood sprinkled on us. It is not primarily man's sign and declaration of his faith, because then we would have to wait until every participant in baptism declares his or her own faith before baptizing. Such a view of baptism is wholly inconsistent with Scripture. Therefore, let nothing keep us from following Jesus by saying, "Permit the children to come to me; do not hinder them; for the kingdom of God belongs to such as these" (Mark 10:14).

> The children of your servants will continue, and their descendants will be established before You.
>
> —Ps. 102:28

> But the lovingkindness of the Lord is from everlasting to everlasting on those who fear Him, and His righteousness to children's children, to those who keep His covenant and remember His precepts to do them.
>
> —Ps. 103:17-18

> My servant David will be king over them, and they will all have one shepherd; and they will walk in My ordinances and keep My statutes and observe them. They will live on the land that I gave to Jacob My servant, in which your fathers lived; and they will live on it, they, and their sons and their sons' sons, forever; and David My servant will be their prince forever. I will make a covenant of peace with them; it will be an everlasting covenant with them. And I will place them and multiply them, and will set My sanctuary in their midst forever.
>
> —Ezek. 37:24-26

> They will not labor in vain, or bear children for calamity; For they are the offspring of those blessed by the Lord, and their descendants with them.
>
> —Isa. 65:23

> As for Me, this is My covenant with them, says the Lord: My Spirit which is upon you, and My words which I have put in your mouth shall not depart from your mouth, nor from the mouth of your offspring, nor from the mouth of your offspring's offspring, says the Lord, from now and forever.
>
> —Isa. 59:21

Should parents have their children baptized? Yes. Suppose you realize you have been disobedient to the Scriptures in not baptizing your children as infants, and now they can no longer be considered infants. Should you still baptize them? Consider an example of this situation when the sign God required was circumcision.

> At that time the Lord said to Joshua, "Make for yourself flint knives and circumcise again the sons of Israel the second time." So Joshua made himself flint knives and circumcised the sons of Israel at Gibeath-haaraloth. This is the reason why Joshua circumcised them: all the people who came out of Egypt who were males, all the men of war, died in the wilderness along the way after they came out of Egypt. For all the people who came out were circumcised, but all the people who were born in the wilderness along the way as they came out of Egypt had not been circumcised. For the sons of Israel walked forty years in the wilderness, until all the nation, *that is,* the men of war who came out of Egypt, perished because they did not listen to the voice of the Lord, to whom the Lord had sworn that He would not let them see the land which the Lord had sworn to their fathers to give us, a land flowing with milk and honey. Their children whom He raised up in their place, Joshua circumcised; for they were uncircumcised, because they had not circumcised them along the way.
>
> —Josh. 5:2-7

The disobedient parents in this passage from the book of Joshua had children between the ages of infancy and twenty years old. Certainly there are many children between the ages of, say, three and twenty who can embrace the covenant promises of God and personally repent and believe in Christ. Whether they do or not does not remove them from under the authority of their parents. If they are still under the authority of Christian parents, the covenant sign should be applied. In Joshua's day, the covenant sign was circumcision, but today it is baptism. As in Joshua's day, parents are not covenant breakers as long as they received and applied the covenant sign. In the New Testament, we have recorded household baptisms for this very reason. Children of all ages may have been in those houses. The question was not whether they had professed faith in Christ; the question was whether their authorities had done so. If the parents had professed faith in Christ, then they were to apply the covenant sign to everyone under their authority. The promise was "for you and your children and for all who are far off, as many as the Lord our God will call to Himself" (Acts 2:39). No one was to be left in limbo because of age. The covenantal sign is necessary as long as the authority is in place. The case of an incorrigible child who has left home would obviously present the opposite.

Some will still ask whether they should wait until their children profess faith in Christ before they are baptized. No. First, this makes baptism all about the child and all about our faith. But baptism is not about our commitment or even our responsiveness. Rather, it is all about God's graciousness. Baptism was designed by God to be God-centered, not man-centered. Second, God specifically reveals through the father of our faith, Abraham, that he wants the covenant sign placed on everyone in our household under our authority whether they profess faith or not.

> "But My covenant I will establish with Isaac, whom Sarah will bear to you at this season next year." When He finished talking with him, God went up from Abraham. Then Abraham took Ishmael his son, and all the servants who were born in his house and all who were bought with his money, every male among the men of

> Abraham's household, and circumcised the flesh of their foreskin in the very same day, as God had said to him. Now Abraham was ninety-nine years old when he was circumcised in the flesh of his foreskin. And Ishmael his son was thirteen years old when he was circumcised in the flesh of his foreskin. In the very same day Abraham was circumcised, and Ishmael his son. All the men of his household, who were born in the house or bought with money from a foreigner, were circumcised with him.
>
> —Gen. 17:21-27

In this passage, God reveals that his covenant will be established with Isaac. God loved Isaac but rejected Ishmael. Nevertheless, he wanted Ishmael circumcised along with every other male under Abraham's authority. Abraham had been told by divine revelation even before Isaac was born that the covenant would be established with Isaac. Thus, he could have argued with God that to put the sign of the covenant on Ishmael was unnecessary. Abraham could have argued that it would be more prudent to wait to see if Ishmael or his servants were inclined to embrace the covenant to be established with Isaac. But he did not, because he knew the covenant sign was about more than our response. He knew it was about God's grace and he knew it should be applied in worship of God. How awesome it is to love a God who loves our children in a very particular and beneficial way!

Discussion and Study Questions

1. Why do you think the idea of baptism extending to the children of believers seems like a strange ritual to some of God's people?
2. Explain how the salvation of one member of a non-Christian family affects the rest of the family from God's perspective—especially when the leading family member is the one who receives Christ.
3. Do you think God wants to treat the children of the church the same as those in the pagan society? Why or why not?

4. After studying all of the New Testament baptisms as referenced in the above chart, what do you make of the fact that not once do we see an adult being baptized in the presence of his or her family without the whole family being baptized?
5. Mark 10:14-16 reads, "Permit the children to come to me; do not hinder them; for the kingdom of God belongs to such as these. Truly I say to you, whoever does not receive the kingdom of God like a child will not enter it at all. And He took them in His arms and began blessing them, laying His hands on them." What is meant by these verses? Why did Jesus need to say these words? What were the disciples failing to understand in this situation?
6. Compare Genesis 17:7-14, Isaiah 59:21, and Acts 2:38-39. What are the differences, similarities, and implications that God is revealing?
7. "For the promise is for you and your children and for all who are far off, as many as the Lord our God will call to Himself." Explain how the promise of receiving the Holy Spirit in Acts 2:39 does not automatically imply receiving the Holy Spirit in a regenerative sense.
8. Discuss the progressive and ascending work of the Holy Spirit in universal common grace, general common grace, and covenant common grace as it relates to a proper interpretation of 1 Corinthians 7:14.
9. Suppose you realize you have been disobedient to the Scriptures in not baptizing your children as infants, and now they can no longer be considered infants. Should you still baptize them? Why or why not?

Chapter 6

Objections to Baptizing Infants

I AM RELATED to church members who belong to Baptist, Episcopalian, United Methodist, Church of God, and Presbyterian churches. How interesting. We all agree that the Bible teaches us to baptize believers, but we come to baptism from significantly different perspectives. Those from a Reformed emphasis are confident in the need to baptize believers and the infants of believers, and the rest typically have reasons for not baptizing infants. What reasons are usually put forth for not baptizing infants?

Every Baptism Requires Faith before Baptism

"The biblical order is believe first and then be baptized." I have heard this statement many times from godly brothers and sisters in Christ who I know have read their Bibles. First a person believes in Christ, and then he is to be baptized. It is not complicated. I know that those making this statement are sincere and definitely are not deliberately seeking to deceive me or anyone else. But the statement simply is not true. Does the Bible really say faith always precedes baptism? If faith always precedes the ceremony of baptism, then it obviously could not be given to infants since infants would be incapable of exercising saving faith. Are infants unable to possess saving faith?

The immersionist will typically point to passages of Scripture like Acts 2:38, "Repent, and each of you be baptized in the name of Jesus Christ for the forgiveness of your sins; and you will receive the gift of the Holy Spirit," and Mark 16:16, "He who has believed and has been baptized shall be saved; but he who has disbelieved shall be condemned." They say these passages establish the proper order of faith in Christ first, *and then* baptism. There is no objection from anyone who holds to the legitimacy of infant baptism that for unsaved *adults* a credible testimony of faith in Christ is required prior to baptism.

The difference between the immersionist who only wants to baptize after faith and those who will baptize infants of believers prior to the infants' saving faith is in understanding passages like those mentioned above in light of their immediate context, as well as in the context of the Bible as a whole. These passages should not be taken as universal principles for every case of baptism, for they do not address every case of baptism. To interpret them as all-inclusive principles causes conflict with other Scripture passages.

For example, there are passages of Scripture where baptism occurs prior to repentance, and it would be wrong to ignore them as if they do not exist:

> And all were baptized into Moses in the cloud and in the sea; and all ate the same spiritual food; and all drank the same spiritual drink, for they were drinking from a spiritual rock which followed them; and the rock was Christ. Nevertheless, with most of them God was not well-pleased; for they were laid low in the wilderness.
>
> —1 Cor. 10:2-5

> Even Simon himself believed; and after being baptized, he continued on with Philip, and as he observed signs and great miracles taking place, he was constantly amazed. Now when the apostles in Jerusalem heard that Samaria had received the word of God, they sent them Peter and John, who came down

> and prayed for them that they might receive the Holy Spirit. For He had not yet fallen upon any of them; they had simply been baptized in the name of the Lord Jesus. Then they began laying their hands on them, and they were receiving the Holy Spirit. Now when Simon saw that the Spirit was bestowed through the laying on of the apostles' hands, he offered them money, saying, "Give this authority to me as well, so that everyone on whom I lay my hands may receive the Holy Spirit." But Peter said to him, "May your silver perish with you, because you thought you could obtain the gift of God with money! You have no part or portion in this matter, for your heart is not right before God. Therefore repent of this wickedness of yours, and pray the Lord that, if possible, the intention of your heart may be forgiven you. For I see that you are in the gall of bitterness and in the bondage of iniquity." But Simon answered and said, "Pray to the Lord for me yourselves, so that nothing of what you have said may come upon me."
>
> —Acts 8:13-24

Now it is granted that the above passages do not firmly establish an order for what comes first, ritual baptism or repentance. What they do teach us, however, is that the order is not significant—that the timing of baptism is not tied to a prior genuine conversion. In the first passage we are told that all of the Israelites were baptized, and yet God was not pleased with most of them—they were not heaven bound. Their faith in God was false. These were those who drank from the spiritual rock which was Christ, and yet they did not have a genuine profession of faith. But they had been baptized. Their baptism occurred before any genuine repentance.

In the second passage we are introduced to Simon the sorcerer, who claims to believe in Christ, is baptized, and then almost immediately makes known that he is unconverted. It is important to note that the apostles tell him in no uncertain terms what he now needs to do. Notice they do not tell him he needs to repent and be baptized—they only tell him to repent. At this point he had a valid baptism, and yet he was unconverted. What was lacking was repentance and his baptism need not be repeated to follow it. The previous baptism in his unconverted state was sufficient.

Both Mark 16:16 and Acts 2:38 address the very first adult Christians who were publicly converted to Christ and baptized. Since the teaching of Christ was new, no one in the immediate context would have been previously baptized as an infant, or as an adult, for that matter. Infants cannot be baptized until there are some Christian parents. Such is the case on any new mission field. Since the Acts 2 and Mark 16 passages are in the context of new mission field instruction, the commands for children of believers would naturally not come into view. One other way to see this is to see that the context of Mark 16 and Acts 2 is preaching to adults, not children. In 2 Thessalonians 3:10, the preaching is also to adults. Paul proclaims, "For even when we were with you, we used to give you this order: if anyone is not willing to work, then he is not to eat, either." Obviously, this is not preaching to children. We cannot stop feeding our children if they are lazy and have not worked for it. This is an adult context, and Mark 16 and Acts 2 are both in adult contexts as well. They do not command us to postpone the baptism of our children until they provide us with a credible profession of faith.

In Romans 4:9-11, we see that God gave Abraham faith, and we see that the sign and seal of that faith was circumcision:

> Is this blessing then on the circumcised or on the uncircumcised also? For we say, "FAITH WAS CREDITED TO ABRAHAM AS RIGHTEOUSNESS." How then was it credited? While he was circumcised, or uncircumcised? Not while circumcised, but while uncircumcised; and he received the sign of circumcision, a seal of the righteousness of the faith which he had while uncircumcised, so that he might be the father of all who believe without being circumcised, that righteousness might be credited to them.

The apostle Paul teaches that circumcision was not meant to show what nation one belonged to, but rather to show one's relation to faith in God and a work that only God can create in men. In the same way that circumcision pointed to a union with God in the Old Testament, baptism points to a union with God and Christ in the New Testament (Gal. 3:27; Rom. 6:3). The central implication of circumcision and baptism is to signify and seal a union with God and Christ. In Abraham's case, his faith preceded the sign of union with God.

Consider the case of Abraham's son in Genesis 21:4: "Then Abraham circumcised his son Isaac when he was eight days old, as God had commanded him." This passage clearly shows that the *presence* of faith is not necessary for the *sign* of faith. Both circumcision and baptism are *signs* of faith. In the case of adults, such as Abraham, the sign of faith was given *after* faith was present (Rom. 4:9-11). In the case of the infant son Isaac, however, circumcision was given *before* faith was present. The *sign* of faith need not be tied to the *presence* of faith in the child, only in the parent.

My seminary diploma has an official seal on it. It does not signify that I have educated myself, but that the authorities regard me as educated. In a similar way, baptism does not signify and seal that someone has united himself to God, but rather that God regards a union between them that God himself has established. Infant baptism is not to be a mere dedication service of the parents to lead their child biblically, or a mere ceremony of christening where a child is dedicated and given a Christian name. Infant baptism should not be referred to as a dedication or a Christening. It involves more than either of these. The purpose of infant baptism is to show God's grace and union to covenant children. As I have previously said, baptism was not established to demonstrate human responsiveness to God, but to reveal God's graciousness to us. When an infant of believing parents is baptized, the assembly of the saints should be caught up in the worship of God. We should watch in awe as the water is applied to the infant's head, for it is a visible sign that our great and awesome God is stooping to earth to be involved in a covenantal relationship with a little child. How marvelous is the grace of our God! We would be foolish to either ignore or obscure this grace under the guise of a dedication or christening service. When we make baptism about human faith rather than divine grace, we miss the biblical reason for the ritual baptism we are observing. Scripture shows that the children of believers are the recipients of divine grace when God is pleased to grant it to them, and not because they are old enough or repentant enough to receive it.

If one believes infants can die and be saved, they must also believe that those infants have what baptism is a sign and seal of, namely, union with Christ. Without that, no one can be saved (John 14:6). This is not to say that all infants who die are saved, but rather that God can grant salvation since he is the author and furnisher of salvation. It is surprising that some believe an infant can die and go to heaven prior to making a public profession of faith in Christ, and yet they do not also believe that child should have the mark of heaven (baptism) upon him if he is the child of a believer. In other words, such persons are making the mark of heaven more difficult to receive than the reality of heaven. They restrict a child from the sign of heaven, but if the child dies, they comfort the parents by saying the deceased child has what the sign signified.

Does God ever comfort us with examples of infants who are capable of possessing saving faith? Yes indeed. He tells Jeremiah that he was saved, consecrated, and appointed to be a prophet even before he was formed in the womb. "Before I formed you in the womb I knew you, and before you were born I consecrated you; I have appointed you a prophet to the nations" (Jer. 1:5). He tells Zacharias that his son John will be filled with the Holy Spirit while still in his mother's womb. "For he will be great in the sight of the Lord; and he will drink no wine or liquor, and he will be filled with the Holy Spirit while yet in his mother's womb" (Luke 1:15). There are others. Salvation belongs to the Lord!

Finding a few passages of Scripture where faith precedes baptism does not mean it always does, especially since God has provided us with a few verses that reveal baptism before faith, and many passages that reveal circumcision prior to faith. And suggesting that infants are incapable of rightly wearing the sign of baptism is a misunderstanding of the fact that baptism is a sign of God's graciousness toward sinners, and not a sign of a sinner's response to God.

There Are No Biblical Examples of Infant Baptisms

There is no explicit New Testament command in the Bible to baptize children, but that does not mean there is no evidence for infant baptism, and it does not mean the practice is unbiblical. There is no specific command in Scripture to administer the sacrament of the Lord's Supper to women, and there is no specific command in Scripture to celebrate the first day of the week as the Christian Sabbath, but scriptural ground can be found for both of these practices. In the same way, there is scriptural warrant for infant baptism, and thus it should be supported by all Bible believers.

Evidence for its validity can certainly be found in God's Word. Just because there is no specific New Testament command saying children of believing parents must be baptized, that does not mean the command does not exist. It does exist, but you must be a "whole Bible Christian" to understand and observe it. We must be "whole Bible Christians" to obey much of what God has for us, because the New Testament does not always repeat specific Old Testament commands. For example, the second commandment is that "You shall not make for yourself an idol, or any likeness of what is in heaven above or on the earth beneath or in the water under the earth" (Exod. 20:4). There is no place specifically where this command is repeated in the New Testament, but no one would argue against its present day validity. The Old Testament states that we should not curse the deaf or put a stumbling block before the blind (Lev. 19:14). The New Testament never repeats this, but this does not mean we can now curse deaf people and trip the blind. The Old Testament says children are a blessing (Ps. 127:3-5). Since the New Testament does not repeat this, are children now a curse? Obviously not. The sin of bestiality, which is legal grounds for divorce in the Old Testament, is not repeated in the New Testament, yet the abomination clearly remains. What God commands in the Old Testament he does not have to repeat in the New Testament.

Where did we get the idea that the final authority for the Christian life should only be the New Testament Scriptures, thus removing the explicit Old Testament teaching from which infant baptism originates? This practice began during the Anabaptist movement beginning around AD 1523 in Switzerland and AD 1527 in Germany. The Anabaptists were known as the radical or left-wing reformers. They are the ancestors of present day Baptists and Mennonites.

As disciples of Ulrich Zwingli (1484-1531), a pastor in Zurich, the first Anabaptists believed the Reformation was not going far enough fast enough. They separated themselves from Zwingli for more radical reformation by denouncing infant baptism, which had been a practice of the church since the time of the apostles. Other Reformers believed infant baptism was a duty for Christians toward their children in the same way circumcision was a duty for Old Testament believers to their children (Col. 2:11-12). The reasoning here is that since infants were included in the covenant in the Old Testament, they should be included in the New Testament—unless there was explicit teaching to the contrary. In the Old Testament, the children of believers received the covenant sign of circumcision and were included in the covenant promises. This does not have to be repeated in the New Testament for it to be in effect. Just because the sign of the covenant changed from circumcision to baptism does not mean the participants of the covenant changed, unless God says so. As a matter of fact, God does not restrict the participants of the covenant in the New Testament but expands them to include both genders and every ethnic group (Gal. 3:28-29).

The Reformers believed there was continuity between the Old and New Testaments. Most Anabaptists did not agree. They developed a "New Testament only" theology which restricted the application of the Bible. This led to a separatist mentality from society and the denial of the effects of an adult's salvation on their children, who were passive and unaware of the significance of the act of God's grace. Such a narrow view of the Christian life and restricted view of God's covenant relationship with his people were in clear conflict with Reformation principles. Other Reformers criticized the Anabaptist movement for rejecting the principle of *Sola scriptura* (scripture alone) by taking away from the Bible's full authority. The name Anabaptist (or "rebaptizers") was the name given them by their critics, since they insisted on rebaptizing those who came to faith in Christ after the once-for-all sufficient sign of baptism had already been applied to them.

Sadly, many people in our day have continued to propagate the philosophy of building a New Testament church by only using New Testament Scripture. This limits God's church. In Acts 7:38, Stephen clearly considers the Old Testament people God's church. They were just as much God's church as we are. We need to build a biblical church with the use of all of Scripture, not just one-fourth of it.

In Genesis 17:7-12, we have God's everlasting command for covenant parents to apply the sacramental covenant sign to their children:

> "I will establish My covenant between Me and you and your descendants after you throughout their generations for an everlasting covenant, to be God to you and to your descendants after you. I will give to you and to your descendants after you, the land of your sojournings, all the land of Canaan, for an everlasting possession; and I will be their God." God said further to Abraham, "Now as for you, you shall keep My covenant, you and your descendants after you throughout their generations. This is My covenant, which you shall keep, between Me and you and your descendants after you: every male among you shall be circumcised. And you shall be circumcised in the flesh of your foreskin, and it shall be the sign of the covenant between Me and you. And every male among you who is eight days old shall be circumcised throughout your generations, a servant who is born in the house or who is bought with money from any foreigner, who is not of your descendants."

God commanded that the sign and seal of his union with his people be given to his people and to their children as soon as they were eight days old. The thirteenth verse furthermore explicitly states that this is to be an everlasting requirement: "A servant who is born in your house or who is bought with your money shall surely be circumcised; thus shall My covenant be in your flesh for an everlasting covenant." So the Old Testament does have a command that states a sign and seal should be placed on children of the covenant. The New Testament nowhere excludes children from the covenant sign. Instead of saying infant baptism should be excluded, since there are no explicit instances of infant baptism in the New Testament, those making this claim need to reveal an explicit command excluding children from receiving God's covenant sign.

Immersionists say that the sign of the covenant was abrogated with the coming of Christ, but the Scriptures make it clear that it continues in what we now call baptism. In his letter to the Colossians, the apostle Paul reveals that God did not revoke his command to give the sign and seal of the covenant to children; he only changed its form.

> ...and in Him you were also circumcised with a circumcision made without hands, in the removal of the body of the flesh by the circumcision of Christ; having been buried with Him in baptism, in which you were also raised up with Him through faith in the working of God, who raised Him from the dead.
>
> —Col. 2:11-12

We are still given the sign and seal of God's everlasting covenant in what is now called a "circumcision made without hands," namely baptism. And since the sign and seal was applied to children in the Old Testament, it ought also to be applied to children today, since God everlastingly ordained it.

One must realize that, in the New Testament, there is a *continuity* (though not *identity*) with the old covenant. In the old covenant, the covenant sign of circumcision was not only permitted to be administered to infants, it was commanded. The continuity between the old and new covenants keeps this in force today.

For those who require that Old Testament commands be repeated in the New Testament, a brief review of Galatians 3:16-17 is in order:

> Now the promises were spoken to Abraham and to his seed. He does not say, "And to seeds," as referring to many, but rather to one, "And to your seed," that is, Christ. What I am saying is

> this: the Law, which came four hundred and thirty years later, does not invalidate a covenant previously ratified by God, so as to nullify the promise.

This passage makes it clear that we do not need a New Testament command if we already have an Old Testament command, and furthermore what God says in the New Testament does not invalidate what he has said in the Old Testament unless he gives us express notice of such action. The Old Testament, along with Colossians 2:11-12, clearly commands infant baptism. The only way to get around this is to find a New Testament command that forbids it. No one has been able to do this since the New Testament supports the Old Testament command and has never abrogated it.

The New Testament records five different household or whole-family baptisms (Acts 10:22-48; 11:14; 16:14-15; 16:31-34; 18:8; 1 Cor. 1:14, 16). Some would have us believe that because of Acts 16:32, "And they spoke the word of the Lord to him together with all who were in his house," that everyone in every household where baptism occurred were old enough to exercise faith in Christ and did so before they were all baptized together. Though I have never heard of such a thing actually happening in all my years of ministry, I do not doubt that God could give faith to every member of a household all at the same time. But a good reading of household circumcisions might show that children could be baptized by the profession of their parents' faith, since the sign of the covenant is about what God is doing, not about what man is doing.

Baptism Is Biblically Defined as an Act Done Through Faith, and an Appeal to God for a Good Conscience

Those who put forth this argument say that baptism is to be about the participant's faith and not their parent's faith. That is, baptism is to be an outward expression of one's inward faith—either that, or it is not baptism.

> ...and in Him you were also circumcised with a circumcision made without hands, in the removal of the body of the flesh by the

> circumcision of Christ; having been buried with Him in baptism, in which you were also raised up with Him through faith in the working of God, who raised Him from the dead.
>
> —Col. 2:11-12

The assumption here is that union with Christ in baptism, and union with Christ through faith, are always one and the same. The ritual and the reality have the same cause. This gives rise to the view of multiple baptisms, that if the outward faith is not genuinely expressing the inward heart, then another baptism needs to occur when the inward reality of faith is present. This creates a human-centered emphasis running contrary to God's teaching in the case of Simon the sorcerer (Acts 8:9-24).

It is also said that baptism is to be an outward act and expression of an inner confession of need to God for spiritual cleansing—an appeal to God for a clean conscience.

> Corresponding to that, baptism now saves you—not the removal of dirt from the flesh, but an appeal to God for a good conscience—through the resurrection of Jesus Christ.
>
> —1 Pet. 3:21

Obviously young children cannot perform this. The assumptions made are that Peter is not defining ritual baptism but real baptism, and that ritual baptism is a sign of faith from man to God rather than a sign of covenant grace from God to man.

In the third chapter of 1 Peter, the apostle addresses the positive and not the negative side of the flood experience. There were eight people saved and brought safely through the water (3:20). As they were lifted up in the ark, they were leaving a world of iniquity behind. God had carried them in the ark over an ocean full of human corruption. Why are we reminded of this salvation? Because it illustrates the salvation of all who are in Christ. For everyone who embraces Christ and is baptized into Christ is safe, just as Noah was safe in the ark.

Our baptism corresponds to Noah and his family's salvation. Just as the ark saved them, our baptism saves us. How does baptism save us? To understand this we must realize that Peter is not speaking about our outward ritual baptism. He makes this clear by the phrase "not the removal of dirt from the flesh." In other words, he is not talking about simply washing away dirt with water, which is an outward sign of baptism. Rather, he is speaking about the inward spiritual union to Christ symbolized in ritual baptism but only experienced by those who are genuinely saved in Christ.

The eight people saved through the flood waters depict those who have been spiritually baptized into Christ and who have had "an appeal to God for a good conscience—through the resurrection of Jesus Christ." The inward reality to which Peter refers is God cleansing us from all our sin and bringing us to the inward reality of union or baptism with Christ. In other words, Peter is saying the baptism he refers to is an appeal to God for a clean heart, a new life, and a new conscience based on the work of Christ through his resurrection. Since Christ is now victorious after having died and risen again to remove our sin, we must go to God and appeal that his Son's work be applied to our lives. If that happens, then we receive the baptism of the Spirit of God which saves us from our sin. Spirit baptism puts a person into Christ, "into one body …to drink of one Spirit" (1 Cor. 12:13).

The apostle Paul also refers to being "baptized into Christ Jesus" as being united with him and receiving all of his benefits (Rom. 6:3). In Christ we have the benefits of his death, burial, resurrection, and ascension. These benefits guarantee us a new life with Christ in which we are raised up to sit with him in heavenly places (Eph. 2:6; Col. 3:1).

Just as water saved eight people who were in the ark, union with Christ's resurrection lifts us up and saves us from this evil and corrupt world. Just as Noah was saved *in* the ark, we are saved *in* Christ. When we are united to Christ, we enter into his resurrection and are lifted up above all evil demonic angels, spirits, authorities, and powers over this world. Just as Noah's ark buoyed him above the forces opposing God that were drowned in the flood, so our union with Christ's resurrection buoys us above. Just as the flood separated Noah and his family from the wicked world of their day, our spiritual baptism into Christ separates us from our evil world. It is more than removing dirty flesh; it is a removal from sin and evil forces. Union with Christ through baptism into his resurrection is the counterpart of the flood. Just as the ark carried the righteous, so now Christ himself carries the righteous safe from all evil and harm. Let us rejoice in the zeal of Christ to carry us over and above the wickedness of this world.

The question we must ask ourselves is whether or not we have made an appeal to God. Have we sought his presence? Have we pleaded with him to give us a good conscience through the resurrection of Jesus Christ? Have we been seeking merely ritual baptism with God through religious ceremony, or have we genuinely been seeking a new life with Christ—even if it involves suffering? God wants to carry the righteous so that they are as safe as Noah was safe in the ark. He carries only those who have made an appeal for a good conscience through the resurrection of Christ.

If the whole earth were to be destroyed by a flood, Christ would still carry those who are righteous. Should evil forces rise up against us, Christ would be zealous to subdue them. Let us rejoice in the Lord's resurrection and be zealous to live in the spiritual victory that has been gained through it. Many Christians today live as though they are spiritually defeated. They see the world rapidly getting worse and heading to ruination, and they know of nothing to do about it. Their god is extremely small. But Christ is victor and he has announced his victory even to all the evil forces and powers in the heavenly realm. His church is not going to get smaller and smaller. He is building a strong and mighty army. His church will be triumphant because he is already victorious over evil, forces of darkness, death, the grave, and even sin itself.

Let us rejoice in Christ's protection and be zealous to promote the safety which is found through union to the true body and church of Christ. It was Noah and his family that God spared in Noah's day, and it is the church, which Christ purchased with his own blood, which God will spare in our day (Acts 20:28). Above all, we must be sure to be found in the true church of God. Spiritual baptism is seen as union to the covenant community, union to Christ and his people, and through such a union there is eternal safety.

Scripture Does Not Support Baptism Replacing Circumcision as a Sign of the New Covenant

In Acts 15:1-29, the apostles are debating the New Testament value of circumcision. There are some who think that baptism—more specifically, infant baptism—should have been brought up in this debate if, in fact, baptism replaced circumcision. They think that not only should baptism have been brought up, it should have been shown to be valid for both adults and children. But such a view neglects the context. We cannot expect nonissues to be brought up as primary points of a debate. The issue for the Council at Jerusalem in Acts 15 is not whether Jewish Christians should stop including their children in the covenant community until they professed faith in Christ. The issue was whether baptism was enough for Gentile Christians to bring their children into the covenant community. Or did they have to bring them into the covenant community by way of circumcision? And the simple answer was that circumcision would no longer be required.

God had taught much in the Old Testament concerning his desire for his covenant sign to be upon whole households. He had done much preparation through sending John the Baptist to begin baptizing the nations and turning the hearts of fathers to their whole household. When this is understood, we see there is no struggle with accepting baptism for believers and their children. This didn't need to be explained at the Jerusalem Council recorded in Acts chapter fifteen. There was no need to develop a baptism argument at this point since it had already been prophesied (Isa. 52:13-15; Ezek. 36:24-27) and developed with John the Baptist. What they didn't know was whether circumcision needed to continue.

Circumcision, rightly understood, was a promise of the sign and seal of the righteousness of Christ. Baptism is a sign and seal of the righteousness of Christ that has come. The promises have been fulfilled in Christ. Circumcision was the sign directing us forward to Christ, and baptism is the sign directing us back to Christ. They are both about the righteousness we have in Christ. Neither of these signs is about us, what we have done or will do. They do not proclaim that father Abraham got saved; rather, they proclaim that the righteousness of Christ has come to Abraham and his seed. God gave us circumcision and baptism not to point us to those who have been redeemed, but to point us to the Redeemer who is Christ Jesus our Lord. That is beautiful and, when properly seen, reaps many benefits.

Perhaps the primary passage connecting circumcision with baptism is Colossians 2:11-12:

> ...and in Him you were also circumcised with a circumcision made without hands, in the removal of the body of the flesh by the circumcision of Christ; having been buried with Him in baptism, in which you were also raised up with Him through faith in the working of God, who raised Him from the dead.

The apostle Paul is addressing uncircumcised Gentiles and tells them that even though they had not received a physical circumcision, they had received what they needed, namely, baptism in Christ. The baptism he refers to here is not ritual baptism. He is talking about heart circumcision—the heart regeneration which occurs by the Holy Spirit. They had not been born Jews and circumcised, but they had been born again in Christ, and their old hearts were cut away (spiritual circumcision) when they were given new hearts in Christ by the Holy Spirit. This spiritual circumcision is described as occurring when they were buried with Christ in baptism. Can it be any clearer? There is a spiritual baptism which accomplishes a spiritual circumcision.

When Paul describes this circumcision as that which was "made without hands," he avoids any confusion with the physical "cutting of the flesh" circumcision. In the same way, when he describes the baptism as "buried with Him ...raised up with Him through faith in the working of God," he avoids any confusion with the water ritual of baptism. Both the water ritual and the cutting of flesh are performed "with hands." The hands-on ritual of circumcision in the old covenant has been replaced with the hands-on ritual of baptism as the sign of the new covenant. Circumcision of the heart, to which the old covenant sign pointed, has been replaced by union to Christ, to which the new covenant sign of water baptism points. Baptism is not a picture of what the believer or anyone has done with his or her own hands. Baptism is not a picture of the believer's own burial and resurrection. Rather, it is a picture of our union with Christ's burial and resurrection. As the preacher pours and sprinkles out water, it points to Christ pouring out his Spirit and sprinkling his blood for the purpose of union with his people.

In the New Testament era, the people of God received the message that physical circumcision no longer mattered; what mattered was spiritual baptism. Paul put it this way: "For neither is circumcision anything, nor uncircumcision, but a new creation" (Gal. 6:15). This transition from circumcision to baptism was a difficult pill for some of the Jews to swallow since they were so accustomed to circumcision. And this issue was a constant source of persecution for the apostle Paul. In Acts 21, the Jerusalem church elders met with Paul and said that "many thousands" of Jews had been told he was "teaching all the Jews who are among the Gentiles to forsake Moses, telling them not to circumcise their children" (Acts 21:20-21). They went on to say they knew what the thousands of Jews had been told was not true; nevertheless, it was true that the Gentiles did not need to circumcise their children (21:24-26). Why was this true? Because circumcision had been replaced by baptism.

Circumcision would still be in force had baptism not replaced it. Jesus told his disciples to make disciples of every nation and to baptize them, not circumcise them (Matt. 28:19). Both Jew and Gentile alike were to be baptized. It was fine if the Jew wanted to continue with the circumcision ritual, but it was no longer the sign of our covenant union with God. With the expansion of the covenant to every nation came a sprinkling for the nations. Just as Jewish parents of old wanted their whole household circumcised, Christian parents now wanted their whole household baptized. No one was telling the Jewish parents that their infants were excluded from the covenant community until they were older, so why should the Gentile children be excluded? "For the promise is for you *and your children* and for all who are far off, as many as the Lord our God will call to Himself" (Acts 2:39 emphasis added).

There Is No Continuity between the Old Testament People of God and the People of Christ's Church Today—We Have a New Covenant which Only Includes Those Professing Genuine Faith in Christ

Those who argue this perspective do not see a correspondence between circumcision and baptism. They may say, "There seems to be some connection between circumcision and baptism in Colossians 2:11-12, but we only see this for the sake of understanding the argument of reformers. We have heard the argument that baptism replaces circumcision, but we don't buy it. We have heard the argument that the children of believers today belong to the visible church, just like the infants who were circumcised in the Old Testament belonged to the Old Testament church. But in our view, only regenerate people are in the New Covenant, and infants are not regenerate, or we don't know that they are. We should not give the sign of the covenant (baptism) until they publicly profess their faith in Christ."

This argument positions the children of today in an inferior position to the children of the Old Testament. In this sense, it makes the New Covenant inferior to the Old Covenant. What does God say?

> Is this blessing then on the circumcised, or on the uncircumcised also? For we say, "FAITH WAS CREDITED TO ABRAHAM AS RIGHTEOUSNESS." How then was it credited? While he was circumcised, or uncircumcised? Not while circumcised, but while uncircumcised; and he received the sign of circumcision, a seal of the righteousness of the faith which he had while uncircumcised, so that he might be the father of all who believe without being circumcised, that righteousness might be credited to them, and the father of circumcision to those who not only are of the

> circumcision, but who also follow in the steps of the faith of our father Abraham which he had while uncircumcised.
>
> —Rom. 4:9-12

Faith is credited to Abraham as righteousness, and this was done prior to his being circumcised. In other words, Abraham's justification was not brought about through his circumcision—since that came after his justification. He was justified while still uncircumcised. The justification was brought about through the reality of faith and not through the ritual of circumcision, which came after his faith. In this way, Abraham is the father of those who have faith, and the emphasis for the future is on faith and not circumcision. The circumcision of Abraham is only a sign and seal of his faith, but the circumcision was not that which brought about the faith. This ritual was not the reality of his union with Christ.

Paul writes that circumcision is specifically called "the sign ...a seal of the righteousness of the faith which he had." It is understood that this righteousness of faith is the means to the covenant union that Abraham had with God and is established by grace alone. Otherwise, the faith and God's gracious promise is made void and becomes a work of obedience to the law, which it is not. Romans 4:16 says very clearly the faith we are talking about is in accordance with God's grace and is *not* a work of man: "For this reason it is by faith, in order that it may be in accordance with grace, so that the promise will be guaranteed to all the descendants, not only to those who are of the Law, but also to those who are of the faith of Abraham, who is the father of us all."

With that understood, we are left with circumcision and baptism signifying the same thing—union with God through faith by his grace. Notice very clearly that the seal of circumcision was *not* of Abraham's faith. It was a seal of the righteousness he had received by faith. His righteousness was Christ and not his own personal faith. When this is clear, we see that it is wrong to think of his circumcision as his personal testimony, just as it would be wrong to think of one's baptism as their personal testimony. The seal is God's seal of the righteousness of Christ. For Abraham, it was a seal of a promised Christ, and for us, it is a seal of the risen Christ. For both, it is about Christ, not us.

This brings us to the heart of the argument on the continuity between the Old Testament people of God and the Christian church today. Those who say we are wrong to baptize infants say we are wrong to assume a similarity between the two. They argue that the way God constituted his people in the Old Testament is fundamentally different from the way he constitutes his people today. Even though circumcision and baptism are both covenant signs signifying union with God, it was right to give the sign to unbelieving children in the Old Testament but not to give the sign of baptism to the unbelieving children of believers in the New Testament. Something is fundamentally different in the New Testament with the makeup of the people of God, and this fundamental difference is an emphasis on the spiritual Israel (people of God) and not the physical Israel (the national Jewish people of God). Because of this difference, the administration of the covenant sign should change and only be given to the true spiritual Israel (believers in Christ). Since we do not know which ones are the true Israel until they profess their faith in Christ, we must wait on this profession of faith before baptism can be properly applied.

Further, those who oppose baptizing infants argue that in the Old Testament, God clearly marked out whole households prior to them all having faith in him. They were nonetheless his physical, national, ethnic people, and they needed the sign of circumcision to distinguish them as God's people. But in the New Testament, no one needs the sign of the covenant (baptism) until we know them to be believers. God is no longer marking out a national group but is now marking out an international group of true believers. God is gathering his people differently. Before, he gathered them by their nationality, their race, but now he is gathering them by their faith in Christ. This explains why it is fitting to give circumcision to all of the Old Testament Jews, even children, but why it is not fitting to give baptism to infants today. Circumcision and baptism do not have the same role to play. Circumcision was God uniting himself to a particular ethnic group; baptism is God uniting himself to those who are genuinely his through faith alone.

Though this argument may sound biblical, it is flawed, because the differences between the old and new covenant people do not call for a different application of the covenant sign. Nowhere does God tell us to exclude children from receiving the covenant sign. Why then assume there is a different application? This would be creating a new covenant that is more limited and more restrictive than the old covenant. The new covenant expands the old covenant; it does not restrict it.

In the Old Testament, God was surely marking out a national people and administering a national covenant. In the New Testament, he goes international by making disciples of every ethnic group in all nations (Matt. 28:19). This does not require a restrictive application of the covenant sign to adult believers, and it is wrongly assumed that the new covenant, as described by the New Testament, will have only true believers within it. "But it is not as though the word of God has failed. For they are not all Israel who are descended from Israel; nor are they all children because they are Abraham's descendants, but: 'through Isaac your descendants will be named.' That is, it is not the children of the flesh who are children of God, but the children of the promise are regarded as descendants" (Rom. 9:6-8). Therefore, the old covenant had two Israels: the ethnic Israel and the spiritual Israel. The wrong assumption is that the new covenant abandons all physical and ethnic elements to establish a strictly spiritual and regenerate Israel. In reality, we still have two Israels" in the New Testament—those who are physically in the covenant community, and those within the covenant community who are truly spiritually reborn.

Jesus speaks of the New Testament church as having "wheat and tares," genuine fruitful Christians and unfruitful members of the same kingdom who are to grow together until the harvest (Matt. 13:24-30). It would be nice if the present-day kingdom of God were only made up of genuine, recognizable believers. We want it this way and we would like to make it this way by restrictive practices, but Jesus forbids it, knowing that such practices harm the true body of Christ.

In Hebrews 6:4-8, we have church members listed who take part in all the aspects of covenant community life and yet do not end up producing the fruit of eternal life.

> For in the case of those who have once been enlightened and have tasted of the heavenly gift and have been made partakers of the Holy Spirit, and have tasted the good word of God and the powers of the age to come, and then have fallen away, it is impossible to renew them again to repentance, since they again crucify to themselves the Son of God and put Him to open shame. For ground that drinks the rain which often falls on it and brings forth vegetation useful to those for whose sake it is also tilled, receives a blessing from God; but if it yields thorns and thistles, it is worthless and close to being cursed, and it ends up being burned.

In 1 Corinthians 7:14, we have unbelieving children God seeks to sanctify through a believing parent, and God exhorts the believing spouse to be cautious in missing the importance of this ministry within the covenant community.

> For the unbelieving husband is sanctified through his wife, and the unbelieving wife is sanctified through her believing husband; for otherwise your children are unclean, but now they are holy.

In John 15:2-6, Jesus gives us the vine/branch metaphor and describes church members and participants who are "in him" and yet are not "of him," for they will be cast out into the lake of fire.

> Every branch in Me that does not bear fruit, He takes away; and every branch that bears fruit, He prunes it so that it may bear more fruit. You are already clean because of the word which I have spoken to you. Abide in Me, and I in you. As the branch cannot bear fruit of itself unless it abides in the vine, so neither can you unless you abide in Me. I am the vine, you are the branches; he who abides in Me and I in him, he bears much fruit, for apart

> from Me you can do nothing. If anyone does not abide in Me, he is thrown away as a branch and dries up; and they gather them, and cast them into the fire and they are burned.

These are clearly covenant breakers who live within the covenant community. Surely regenerate members of the covenant community are never lost to hell. Therefore, not all the members of the new covenant are regenerate. There are fellow members who will go out from us who are not of us (1 John 2:19), and judgment will begin within the household of God (1 Pet. 4:17). When we read of the seven New Testament churches in the second and third chapters of the book of Revelation, we read of hypocrites in every single church, and five out of seven of them have false teachers in their midst. These are people who strongly profess to know God to the church, and yet are later shown to be without Christ. Jude warns the church today to continue in the faith with the example that, "The Lord, after saving a people out of the Land of Egypt, subsequently destroyed those who did not believe" (Jude 5). The implication being that just because one claims to have come to Christ and has been baptized does not mean they will call heaven their home. We must test ourselves to see if we produce the fruit of genuine faith and repentance. Such is the nature of the new covenant church.

Both old and new covenants have an Israel within an Israel, a visible church within the invisible church, an elect remnant within a larger body. This has not changed. What has changed is that, with the coming of Christ, the larger physical body known as the church is now expanded to include God's mission to every ethnic group. Until Christ returns, there will always be people who wear the sign of union with God (baptism) falsely, both adults and children. I would venture to say that every local church has known adults who gave a testimony of getting baptized and yet only later (after their public profession of faith) do they experience genuine conversion to Christ. One lady joined our church who had been baptized five different times because each church she went to required it. She lived with a false profession of faith through all but two of those baptisms. The sign always pointed to Christ's grace, but she lived as a covenant breaker until there was genuine conversion.

Simon the sorcerer was a baptized member of the covenant community and yet he was an unregenerate covenant breaker (Acts 8:13, 22). Judas Iscariot took the Lord's Supper with the Lord but failed to take the Lord with that supper. He was a covenant participant who was a covenant breaker (Matt. 26:27-28). The new covenant community has far too many examples of unregenerate participation for us to honestly seek to exclude the unregenerate from our theology or practice.

Neither the Old nor New testaments establish the covenant with God through the application of the covenant sign. In other words, God did not design circumcision or baptism as something we choose for the purpose of declaring our faith in God. The signs of the covenant were chosen by God to be applied to us by our parents, or as soon as we receive the good news of Christ to declare his gracious union with us. We are then required to be obedient as covenant keepers or covenant breakers. The Old Testament period is not the only period in history that had covenant breakers, for we have them today.

I have heard people use Galatians 4:22-28 to argue for a different kind of church today from what was in the Old Testament. The text reads,

> For it is written that Abraham had two sons, one by the bondwoman and one by the free woman. But the son by the bondwoman was born according to the flesh, and the son by the free woman through the promise. This is allegorically speaking, for these women are two covenants: one proceeding from Mount Sinai bearing children who are to be slaves; she is Hagar. Now this Hagar is Mount Sinai in Arabia and corresponds to the present Jerusalem, for she is in slavery with her children. But the Jerusalem above is free; she is our mother. For it is written, "REJOICE, BARREN WOMAN WHO DOES NOT BEAR; BREAK FORTH AND SHOUT, YOU WHO ARE NOT IN LABOR; FOR MORE NUMEROUS ARE THE CHILDREN OF THE DESOLATE

> THAN OF THE ONE WHO HAS A HUSBAND." And you brethren, like Isaac, are children of promise.

They say the church is not a mixture of physical church and spiritual church. The new covenant community today is only the Spirit-born community. As Paul says, we are "like Isaac ...children of promise" and not like Ishmael, "according to the flesh." But they forget that Paul was addressing local churches in the region of Galatia whom he called "brethren" (Gal. 1:2) yet who were nevertheless deserting Christ for another gospel (Gal. 1:6). Paul was "perplexed" about the Galatians (Gal. 4:20). As he told them, he was concerned he may "have labored over you in vain" (Gal. 4:11). Some of the Galatians were living according to the "flesh" and not according to the "Spirit" (Gal. 5:16-26). They would consequently reap eternal corruption, but others would reap eternal life. Paul taught that "whatever a man sows, this he will also reap. For the one who sows to his own flesh will from the flesh reap corruption, but the one who sows to the Spirit will from the Spirit reap eternal life. Let us not lose heart in doing good, for in due time we will reap if we do not grow weary. So then, while we have opportunity, let us do good to all people, and especially to those who are of the household of the faith" (Gal. 6:7-10).

This was the church of Paul's day, and it is just as much the local church experience of our day. There is always a mixture of true and false believers, and always a mixture of "children of the flesh" and "children of God." Nowhere does God call us to sort this all out (as though we could know with certainty the elect) and make sure we only give baptism to the "children of God."

The body of Christ is no longer based on one ethnic group, but is expanded to every group across the world. And just as in the Old Testament, the true church in any ethnic group, whether Jews or some other group, truly belong to God by grace alone. Nothing has changed here that requires us to be more restrictive in the application of the covenant sign. There is certainly no teaching from God saying our children no longer matter to him like they did in the Old Testament, and so it is not fitting for them to receive the covenant sign. God still views the children of believers as the offspring of those he has purchased with his own blood. They are different than the children of those outside the church community (much more on this in the following chapter).

Before we leave the old covenant and new covenant argument, we must deal with some very important passages from the prophet Jeremiah and the book of Hebrews.

> "Behold, days are coming," declares the Lord, "when I will make a new covenant with the house of Israel and with the house of Judah, not like the covenant which I made with their fathers in the day I took them by the hand to bring them out of the land of Egypt, My covenant which they broke, although I was a husband to them," declares the Lord. "But this is the covenant which I will make with the house of Israel after those days," declares the Lord, "I will put My law within them and on their heart I will write it; and I will be their God, and they shall be My people. They will not teach again, each man his neighbor and each man his brother, saying, 'Know the Lord,' for they will all know Me, from the least of them to the greatest of them," declares the Lord, "for I will forgive their iniquity, and their sin I will remember no more."
>
> —Jer. 31:31-34

> For if that first covenant had been faultless, there would have been no occasion sought for a second. For finding fault with them, He says, "Behold, days are coming, says the Lord, when I will effect a new covenant with the house of Israel and with the house of Judah; not like the covenant which I made with their fathers on the day when I took them by the hand to lead them out of the land of Egypt; for they did not continue in my covenant, and I did not care for them," says the Lord, "For this is the covenant that I will make with the house of Israel after those days," says the Lord: I will put my laws into their minds, and I will write them on their hearts. And I will be their God, and they shall be my people. And they shall not teach everyone his fellow citizen, and everyone his brother, saying, 'Know the Lord,' for all will know me, from the least to the greatest of them. For I will be merciful to their iniquities, and I will remember their sins no more." When He said, "A new covenant," He has made the first

> obsolete. But whatever is becoming obsolete and growing old is ready to disappear.
>
> —Heb. 8:7-13

Some assert from these passages that the sign of the covenant (baptism) should be restricted to those who "know the Lord." And since we cannot know whether infants "know the Lord," then they should not be baptized. As we study these passages, we will see again that the new covenant does not restrict infants from membership and its privileges. Furthermore, a right understanding of these passages encourages the baptism of infants within the family of believers.

The prophecies included above regarding the new covenant are like other prophecies of this nature in that they have a "now but not yet" character. The new covenant has come with the first coming of Christ and is continuing with the present reign of Christ, but it will not reach its final completion and fullness until the second coming of Christ. Let us look at several aspects of this.

First, the new covenant will not need to be discarded because of God's people breaking it as before. It has already been fulfilled in Christ, it is being fulfilled in his church through our "filling up what is lacking in Christ's afflictions" (Col. 1:24). It will be completely realized when Christ returns. When we see Jesus face-to-face, it will no longer be possible to break his covenant again, nor will it be possible for any parts of his church to be carried off into exile as they were in Jeremiah's day. Until the new covenant reaches its consummation in Christ, it is still possible to be known as a covenant breaker. This is why there are warnings in the New Testament against breaking the covenant (1 Cor. 10:1-33; Heb. 10:28-31). These warnings would not be there if they were not real.

The New Testament reveals that new covenant community members will continue to break the covenant, and we have all witnessed the reality of this in our own sinful lives. To say that the covenant sign only applies to covenant keepers would ultimately eliminate everybody, not just infants. We all fall miserably short of God's requirements (Rom. 3:23). No matter how strong our faith, we still cry out as Paul did, "Wretched man that I am! Who will set me free from the body of this death? Thanks be to God through Jesus Christ our Lord! So then, on the one hand I myself with my mind am serving the law of God, but on the other, with my flesh the law of sin" (Rom. 7:24-25). Now we are being renewed day by day and have the responsibility to renew ourselves through God's truth and present ourselves to him, which is our spiritual service of worship (Rom. 12:1-2). When we see Jesus, we will be like him (1 John 3:2), and we will find the completion of Jeremiah's prophecy—God's law on our heart and our hearts perfectly consumed with joy in his ways (1 Thess. 3:13; Jude 24-25).

Again, it would be wrong to restrict the new covenant to believers alone. The New Testament has numerous warnings to the covenant community to continue growing in Christ and not fall away. We will not realize the complete fulfillment of the covenant until Christ returns. When this does happen, he will separate the true believers from the false, the sheep from the goats, and the wheat from the tares (Matt. 25:31-46). As fellow-members of the covenant community, we are called to faithful perseverance (1 Cor. 9:27; 2 Cor. 13:5; 2 Pet. 1:10; Rev. 2:7, 11, 17, 26; 3:5, 12, 21; 21:7).

God put children in his covenant community in the days of Abraham and has never taken them out. We should not seek to exclude whom God has included.

> I will establish My covenant between Me and you and your descendants after you throughout their generations for an everlasting covenant, to be God to you and to your descendants after you.
>
> —Gen. 17:7

No Reasons Not To Baptize Infants

We have looked at some of the primary arguments used to not baptize infants and limit the grace of God to only adults, and we have found them insufficient. We have asked, if children are in the covenant community, then what forbids them from receiving the sign of the covenant? The declarations are explicit that the kingdom of God includes children (Matt. 19:14; Mark 10:14; Luke 18:16), the church includes children (1 Cor. 7:14; Eph. 6:1-4; Col. 3:20-21), the covenant promises include children (Deut. 30:6; Jer. 31:36-37; Acts 2:39); and the pattern of household baptisms certainly supports the place of children within the covenant community. Who are we to turn away the "godly offspring" from the sign of the covenant (Mal. 2:15)? Who are we to deny "the gift of the Lord ...the fruit of the womb," which is God's reward (Ps. 127:3)?

Discussion and Study Questions

1. Both 1 Corinthians 10:2-5 and Acts 8:13-24 describe a ritual baptism performed by the people of God where it becomes clear afterwards that some of the participants were not genuinely repented believers. Such passages establish that the timing of baptism is not tied to a prior genuine conversion. Is there a human pride element to either accepting this or not accepting this as true? Explain.
2. Three passages are important to get a better picture of the baptism performed by Moses on the people of God in the wilderness. First Corinthians 10:2-5 is important to observe that it happened. Exodus 24:7-8 is important to see how it happened, and Hebrews 9:19-22 is important to see again that God calls what happened a baptism by sprinkling. Since most of those baptized were not genuine repentant believers, did God mess up and baptize before a genuine faith was evident? Did God prescribe any kind of rebaptism for those who needed it? Why did God allow baptism for some he knew were not repentant?
3. Describe how and why Mark 16:16 and Acts 2:38 do not command us to postpone the baptism of our children until they provide us with a credible profession of faith.
4. In the case of Abraham's son in Genesis 21:4, why is it that the *presence* of faith in Isaac is not necessary for the *sign* of faith? Where is the faith in this passage?

5. Why is it that the sacrament of infant baptism should not be called a "Baby Dedication" or a "Child Christening" service?
6. Is it strange from your perspective that some believe an infant can die and go to heaven prior to making a public profession of faith in Christ, and yet do not also believe the same child should have the mark of heaven (baptism) upon him if he is the child of a believer?
7. What principles must one develop or abandon to deny children entrance into the covenant community through baptism and to require their rebaptism should they come to faith and repentance in Christ later in life?
8. How does Colossians 2:11-12 and Genesis 17:7-12 connect the New Testament baptism with the Old Testament rite of circumcision, and why is this important?
9. Is the baptism reference in 1 Peter 3:21 a reference to a "real" baptism or to a "ritual" baptism, and why does this make a difference?
10. Is there any teaching from God saying our children no longer matter to him like they did in the Old Testament and should therefore not receive the covenant sign? List verses on either side of this issue and explain their instruction.

Chapter 7

Beautiful Benefits for Parents and Their Children

INFANT BAPTISM IS often treated like a ritualistic facade that covers a child without really adding any substantive blessing or significance to him, the parents, or their church family. This attitude is distressing in light of what baptism has to offer.

While teaching a class on the mode of baptism, one man said to me, "It makes no difference what view people take regarding the subject of baptism, especially infant baptism, since baptism never does anyone any good. It doesn't matter how much water is used or how old the person is that is baptized. Baptism doesn't do him any good. Spiritual regeneration is the only thing that changes a person. Religious sacraments only make hypocrisy possible. They dress people up religiously, but do nothing to change their living." I share this man's distaste for religious or sacramental veneer, but not his uninformed opinion that infant baptism has no real spiritual benefits simply because some people have not been living the deep genuine beauty of baptism.

Many people have read the Bible but have received little or nothing of life-changing value from it. Many people attend church services without any apparent life-changing advantage. It wouldn't be wise to tell them to never read the Bible or to quit attending church just because they have yet to see fruit from it. Perhaps the problem is a lack of faith. Hebrews 11:6 tells us, "Without faith it is impossible to please Him, for he who comes to God must believe that He is and that He is a rewarder of those who seek Him." In order to receive the proper benefits through church services, Bible reading, or infant baptism, we must mix faith with it. We must trust God first and foremost, and not just his benefits.

Sadly, many people are focused on what other people are doing during the baptism of infants and have missed the benefits that God willingly gives. Infant baptism was not designed to draw our attention to cute "Kodak moments." It was not designed to draw our attention to the preacher, the parents, the babies, or those who sit in the church congregation. Baptism is designed to be a beautiful and beneficial message and ministry sent down from God as a gift of grace revealing his wonderful relationship with us and our children. It provides us with the opportunity to enjoy all the benefits of this relationship and fulfill our relationship obligations, with thanks to Jesus Christ. To understand baptism's significance and to receive its rich blessings, the focus must always be on divine graciousness and never on human responsiveness.

How many baptisms have we sat through without reaping reward? This should never be. Let us evaluate our focus. Is it man-ward or God-ward? When we begin focusing on what God is saying to us, doing for us, lavishing on us, and desiring for us in baptism, we become overwhelmed by his grace and mercy.

Infant baptism is a rich means of God's grace. Let us not minimize or underestimate its potency. It is tremendously good for our souls if we understand it rightly. Let us therefore study with great eagerness to see all the good God intended us to reap when the sacrament of baptism is applied to our children.

Cautions against Corruption

Many people see the benefits of infant baptism in regeneration, dedication commitments, christening, or some sort of presumptive grace. But the benefits of infant baptism are not to be found in any of these things. Such views corrupt the biblical doctrine of infant baptism and lead us away from its true rewards.

Caution # 1: Baptism regenerates

Infant baptism should not be viewed as a service guaranteeing a child's regeneration by the Spirit of God. There are those who believe children are magically regenerated by God when the water of baptism falls upon them. They view baptism as justification—a cleansing from original human sin and being made right with God. As such, it is transference into the kingdom of God. This view is espoused by Catholics, some Episcopalians, Methodists, Presbyterians, and others. In this view, being baptized is being rescued from one's bondage to sin and God's wrath. Thus, baptism becomes a way we can secure our own salvation. This view is clearly contrary to what the Bible teaches as salvation by grace alone through faith in Christ alone—a salvation that allows us to boast only in God's gift of graciousness and not in our own works (Eph. 2:7-9). To the contrary, baptism is not a guarantee of salvation, and it is not even a presumption of a guarantee of salvation. Salvation is purely a gift offered by God's work and grace alone.

Caution # 2: Baptism Presumes Future Salvation

Just as infant baptism should not be viewed as that which saves, it should also not be viewed as that which promises a certain future salvation without exception. Some believe that infant baptism presumes our children will be saved unless the children somehow demonstrate a denouncing of Christ. Such a view removes any need to evangelize them. If baptism presumes future salvation, our task would be to have our children baptized and living morally acceptable lives. That way there would be no need for any other work of God to have them eternally approved for heaven. For some people, this view arises out of a limited understanding of the command to parents to nurture and admonish their children. They limit the child's need to only what the parents are commanded to provide in Ephesians 6:4, which is bringing them up in the discipline and instruction of the Lord.

This view wrongly assumes that disciplining and instructing excludes the activity of evangelism regarding our children. In other words, since God's commands to parents do not include the command to win their children to Christ, the child must have escaped the need for salvation through baptism. Infant baptism should not be viewed as an ironclad guarantee that through nurture and admonition God is going to save the baptized infant in the future.

There is a presumptive element in the baptizing of infants that brings much comfort, but it should not be equated with presumptive regeneration. What infant baptism does presume is that we who have been baptized are in God's covenant community. Though this does not guarantee salvation, it is much better than living outside God's covenant community. By way of clarification, being included in the *community* of the elect is not the same as being included in the *number* of the elect. Baptism does the former, and we cannot rightly presume on the latter. Through baptism we gain covenant community membership—we become one of the branches of the God-vine mentioned in the fifteenth chapter of John. We are soberly warned, however, that even though we are a part of God—as a branch is connected to its vine—without fruitfulness, the branch is cut off and burned (John 15:1-7). Some in the Old Testament were baptized into Moses and drank from the spiritual rock of Christ, and yet were then laid low by the wrath of God and cut off from his pleasure (1 Cor. 10:2-5). Thus, we would be unwise to presume upon saving grace because of our baptism.

Caution #3: A dedication service can be a good alternative to infant baptism.

Infant baptism was not designed by God to reveal a child's or his parent's dedication to the Lord. Many have used Hannah's dedication of her son Samuel to the Lord as support for this belief (1 Sam. 1:28). But the story of Hannah and Samuel reveals a boy who was given to the priest to live with him and minister to the Lord before him the rest of his days. Nothing in the Scripture encourages anyone else to do likewise. It is nowhere linked to infant baptism or to parental responsibilities.

Every parent should be committed to train up their children in the ways of the Lord, but baptism was not designed to honor parents for this dedication. It was not created to show that parents were interested in their children, but rather to show that God was interested in the children. If my children were to die today, my interest in them would not matter as significantly as God's interest in them. Baptism shows that the greater interest is with God and leads us to worship and blessing. It is only because of God's interest in us and our children that we should naturally respond with dedication to his service and glory. There is nothing sinful about holding dedication services, but they should not be equated with or used as an alternative to a baptism service; they are not the same thing, and they do not have the same focus.

Caution #4: A christening service can be a good alternative to infant baptism.

Infant baptism services have been called christening services, and many christening services may have been baptism services wrongly named. To christen means to name something or someone for Christ's glory. We can christen houses, boats, automobiles, or other possessions, and thus dedicate them for use in Christ's kingdom by giving them Christian names. Yet infant baptism and christening are not one and the same. We do not find the command to christen babies or believers anywhere in the Bible. To associate christening and infant baptism is to distort their true meaning. Unfortunately, many people have adopted a brand of cultural Christianity that allows them to change many biblical terms to their own liking so as to make the obligations to God's Word more palatable to their rebellious souls. They have changed the name of iniquity to infirmity, wickedness to weakness, adultery to "having an affair," lust to love, and baptism to christening. This makes baptism something people do exclusively and leaves God out of the picture. The term for christening is not a biblical one; it is a human invention, and when used in reference to infant baptism, it is a corruption of biblical doctrine.

Comforts for Christians

We do not have to invent false benefits for the doctrine of infant baptism. God designed this sacrament to be a rich means of grace, and when rightly understood, it truly nourishes the souls of parents who baptize their children, the children who grow up being taught that the sign and seal of baptism has been applied to them, and the covenant community who observe the sacrament as it is administered. What follows is a brief description of some of those beautiful and beneficial blessings Christians receive through infant baptism. These are the reasons all Christians should want to have their children baptized.

Benefit #1: To enjoy the smile of God as his obedient child

The emotion of anger draws attention. Whenever you see someone fuming and fussing at the convenience store or in a shopping mall, it grabs your attention. If you see someone who is "steamed," you can't help but notice them. What is it that has caused them to let their blood boil? The disciples must have indelibly noticed the Lord's indignation when he vented his frustration with them for refusing to let the little children come to him in Mark 10:13-16. Jesus said, "Permit the children to come to Me; do not hinder them; for the kingdom of God belongs to such as these."

The Scripture tells us that Jesus was indignant. Indignation is anger over injustice. He was very displeased, righteously so, over the injustice being done to children. The disciples were leaders of God's covenant people, and yet they had failed to understand and apply God's covenant concern for children. Surely they learned never again to invoke the righteous anger of Christ. Have you ever considered how not bringing your children to Christ for blessing can lead God to be angry with you?

Moses was one who provoked the same kind of anger from God in Exodus 4:24-26. Moses and Zipporah had neglected to place the sign and seal of the covenant on their son, and they knew it. Since their children were half-breeds, perhaps they wanted to wait until they were older and professed their own faith in following God before they put the covenant sign on them. Whatever the case, God intended to deal with their sin—by death, unless they quickly repented. Sins unto death are serious matters, and not all sins fall into such a serious category. Consider the righteous anger of God. What if we had lived in Moses' day and refused to have the sign of the covenant placed on our children? Moses found out that applying the covenant sign was not some cute ritual that could be considered optional for believers. The neglect of this sacrament was a heinous sin worthy of death. God was not pleased that Moses was going to Egypt to speak of deliverance by a covenant-keeping God while hypocritically not trusting this God to care for his own children by having them marked out with his covenant sign.

On January 18, 1525, the city council of Zurich issued a command that all parents must baptize their infants within eight days of birth or be thrown out of town. The reformer, Ulrich Zwingli, convinced the town council through debate that infant baptism was a biblical safeguard from the chastening of God. They did not want God's wrath on their town and took heed to the preacher's admonition to have their children baptized.

No one will likely run us out of town if we fail to baptize our children. But we do need to understand that since God has commanded it, it would be a sin for us to neglect it. Just as the city council of Zurich did not want unbaptized people in their town, God does not want unbaptized people in the kingdom of Christ, either. To tell our children or others that they need to believe in God and his promises, but fail to show our own obedience by placing the sign of God's promises on our children, is a hypocritical act that infuriates our covenant-keeping God. The sacraments God has left for his church are not insignificant rituals of no consequence. Just as many have become weak, sick, and even died over a wrong application or neglect of the Lord's Supper, so many incur God's righteous indignation over their improper application or neglect of infant baptism (1 Cor. 11:29-30; Exod. 4:24-26). Abuses of either of the two sacraments of the church fall into the category of sins unto death. The extensive example and warning in 1 Corinthians 10:1-12 is to show us how deathly serious God is about our right application of baptism and the Lord's communion. Those Old Testament Jews who held their wilderness baptism and table of communion with contempt experienced death and the displeasure of God; blessings were only for the faithful. As for me, I prefer to learn from their example and not live in such a manner as to invoke God's displeasure.

Benefit #2: To know more completely the love of God for families

From God's creation of the Garden of Eden, it is clear that he not only wanted to establish the family unit but also provide for it. In Genesis 6:8-9, we find that God walked with Noah because Noah was a righteous and blameless man. Noah found favor with God, and yet God doesn't save only Noah, he saves his entire household during the tragic flood. A brief survey of redemptive events in Scripture shows consistent concern from God for families, not just individuals. When God redeemed his people out of Egypt, he promised them that he would spare entire households if they would in faith apply the blood of the Passover lamb to their homes (Exod. 12:3). Clearly God's concern is not just for the parents or individuals in a household. His concern is for whole households, wherever a believer resides.

In the New Testament, God's concern for families continues. When Paul preached the gospel to women gathered by the river, the woman named Lydia was saved and she and her entire household were baptized (Acts 16:14-15). The Scripture only reveals the heart change of Lydia, yet her whole household was baptized. The same is true of the Philippian jailer. He was saved, yet his whole family was baptized (Acts 16:31-34). We do not know if his entire family had faith in Christ, or the ages of any of the family members. All we know is that God's concern was to baptize the entire family.

Over and over again, God deals with covenant families in similar fashion. In 1 Corinthians 1:14-16, Paul tells us he baptized the household of Stephanus. This passage says nothing about the beliefs of the members of the Stephanus household, but God's covenant promises extended to everyone in it. In 1 Corinthians 7:14, God declares that the unsaved children of believing parents are not to be reckoned as part of the world, but rather as part of the church. They are to be considered as God's holy ones, for God is concerned not only for believers, but also for their entire household.

The concept of God's covenant love as seen through the covenant sign of circumcision, and now baptism, began with God's covenant to Abraham in Genesis 17:7, 11-12:

> I will establish My covenant between Me and you and your descendants after you throughout their generations for an everlasting covenant, to be God to you and to your descendants after you.... And you shall be circumcised in the flesh of your foreskin, and it shall be the sign of the covenant between Me and you. And every male among you who is eight days old shall be circumcised throughout your generations, a servant who is born in the house or who is bought with money from any foreigner, who is not of your descendants.

In this passage, God promises not only to be the God of the believer, but also the God of the believer's children. Our children are not to be treated as pagans waiting to choose a god. Notice God declares that the children of believers have this covenant love relationship with him even before their birth. And this relationship with God is not short term, for God declared it to be an everlasting covenantal love. The sign of circumcision was to remind the parent as well as the children that God had marked them out to receive his special love. Through the cutting involved in circumcision, God was demonstrating that he had cut away the sin and offense of his people and reconciled them to himself. What a glorious demonstration of his love.

The covenant sign of circumcision was replaced in the New Testament with the covenant sign of baptism. Since the bloody sacrifice of Jesus was once for all sufficient to pay for our sins, God does away with the bloody sign and replaces it with a sign of cleansing through water. "In Him you were also circumcised with a circumcision made without hands, in the removal of the body of the flesh by the circumcision of Christ; having been buried with Him in baptism, in which you were also raised up with Him through faith in the working of God, who raised Him from the dead" (Col. 2:11-12). Jews were saying that Gentile believers needed to be circumcised in order to be fully saved. But God revealed to the apostle Paul that what is needed is only to be baptized into Christ—and not to be circumcised. Our baptism is now the sign that the blood of Christ is spiritually applied to us, just as water is ritually applied to us to cleanse us from our sin and to unite us to our God.

God's promises of love for entire families seen through the sacrament of baptism are undeniable. In Galatians 3:29, we are told that if we belong to Christ, then we are Abraham's seed and "heirs according to promise." In other words, God's design all along was to save families, not just some families, but families related to the covenant promise. God's loving concern is to save generations. Consider his undeniable, loving promises:

> As for Me, behold, My covenant is with you, And you will be the father of a multitude of nations. "No longer shall your name be called Abram, But your name shall be Abraham; For I have made you the father of a multitude of nations. I will make you exceedingly fruitful, and I will make nations of you, and kings will come forth from you. I will establish My covenant between Me and you and your descendants after you throughout their generations for an everlasting covenant, to be God to you and to your descendants after you.
>
> —Gen. 17:4-7

> Know therefore that the Lord your God, He is God, the faithful God, who keeps His covenant and His lovingkindness to a thousandth generation with those who love Him and keep His commandments.
>
> —Deut. 7:9

> The children of Your servants will continue, And their descendants will be established before You.
>
> —Ps. 102:28

> But the lovingkindness of the Lord is from everlasting to everlasting on those who fear Him, And His righteousness to children's children, To those who keep His covenant And remember His precepts to do them.
>
> —Ps. 103:17-18

> "As for Me, this is My covenant with them," says the Lord: "My Spirit which is upon you, and My words which I have put in your mouth shall not depart from your mouth, nor from the mouth of your offspring, nor from the mouth of your offspring's offspring," says the Lord, "from now and forever."
>
> —Isa. 59:21

> My servant David will be king over them, and they will all have one shepherd; and they will walk in My ordinances and keep My statutes and observe them. They will live on the land that I gave to Jacob My servant, in which your fathers lived; and they will live on it, they, and their sons and their sons' sons, forever; and David My servant will be their prince forever. I will make a covenant of peace with them; it will be an everlasting covenant with them. And I will place them and multiply them, and will set My sanctuary in their midst forever. My dwelling place also will be with them; and I will be their God, and they will be My people.
>
> —Ezek. 37:24-27

> For the promise is for you and your children and for all who are far off, as many as the Lord our God will call to Himself.
>
> —Acts 2:39

God's love is not just for us, but it is for our children and our children's children. As the *water* sprinkles down upon the heads of our children, let us see a demonstration of the passing down of God's love to them as well. God's love does not start from scratch with each new birth or generation. He has promised us love that extends "to a thousand generations" (Deut. 5:10; 7:9; Ps. 103:17; Eph. 6:1-4). God has a passion to save entire households. To him be praise and glory.

Benefit #3: To know more completely the love of God for children

Though we cannot have certain knowledge of our child's salvation while an infant, we can know that they are set apart at baptism to be viewed differently by God. According to 1 Corinthians 7:14, "the unbelieving husband is sanctified through his wife, and the unbelieving wife is sanctified through her believing husband; for otherwise your children are unclean, but now they are holy." God sees a covenant child as holy, and those who are not covenant children are seen as unclean. The cleansing water symbolized in baptism sets our children apart for life in the covenant community and distinguishes them from those in the world who have yet to experience special sanctifying grace from God. God demonstrates for us that he loves our children as his own covenant children. What a tremendous comfort!

Because I was the son of the owner of a business, I received several jobs in life. I received other jobs because I was the friend of the son of the owner. There are wonderful benefits in being related to the owner, or being friends with a relative of the owner. Just ask those who don't have this privilege. Baptism does not make us sons of God, but it does mean we are related to the sons of God. Everyone knows that is much better than being total strangers. In baptism we are not yet given the status of son or heir, but we are given the status of friend and relative of a friend, which is much better than the status of a stranger. The friends of God receive the attention and ministry of God in a way strangers do not. Baptism removes our children from the category of being foreigners and strangers to God.

Though our children may still be non-Christians and by nature hostile to God (Rom. 8:7-8), it is extremely comforting to know that in that condition God will view them through their baptism as those children to whom he desires to express his covenantal love that leads to the salvation for all the elect. Do we not know that "the kindness of God leads you to repentance?" (Rom. 2:4). Do we think lightly of such kindness?

Benefit # 4: To faithfully declare the ownership of God for our stewardship

When the sacrament of baptism is rightly being performed on our children, God is doing something. He is providing us with a safeguard from his righteous indignation and chastisement. He is demonstrating his love for our families and, in particular, his love for our children. There is more. Our God is declaring his ownership for our stewardship. He is declaring that our children are his children, and they have the responsibility to behave as such. In what sense are our children God's children? Children of believers are God's covenant servants, not in the sense of being regenerate servants, for this is only their status when he grants them faith and repentance, but they are servants nevertheless.

Since infant baptism is only to be applied to the children of believers, it implies a prior work on God's part. It implies that God has been at work granting faith and repentance in Jesus Christ to at least one of the parents of the candidates for baptism. We know that faith and repentance are God's gracious gifts to sinners for our salvation (Eph .2:8-9; 2 Tim. 2:25-26). We also know that the reason God can justly give us these gracious gifts is because Jesus Christ has purchased our right to them by his own redeeming sacrifice. The Scripture says, "Do you not know that your body is a temple of the Holy Spirit who is in you, whom you have from God, and that you are not your own? For you have been bought with a price: therefore glorify God in your body" (1 Cor. 6:19-20). Elsewhere God describes the church as that "which He purchased with His own blood" (Acts 20:28). When Christ purchased us, we became his bondservants, and as his servants we bring to him and serve him with all that we have, even our own children. This matter of ownership of all that is ours coming under the purchase by Christ is declared through baptism.

Suppose I purchase several chickens for the purpose of supplying my family with fresh eggs. When the chickens lay their eggs, then whose eggs are they? Do the eggs belong to the chicken or do the eggs belong to the owner of the chicken? If I let some of the eggs hatch, do the new chickens belong to the momma chicken, or do they belong to the owner of the chickens? The answer is obvious. Not only do the eggs belong to me, but the chicken's children belong to me for a thousand generations. The chickens have been bought with a price. Therefore, they are under obligation to honor me and to give over their eggs and their little chickens to my ownership.

Since baptism has replaced circumcision (Col. 2:11-12), and since we were commanded to circumcise our children and declare them to be God's own covenant people (Gen. 17:6-13), baptism is God at work declaring his ownership. He has not only purchased us with his own blood, but he has claimed the right to our children. The parent who says, "I am going to let my children choose for themselves when they are baptized," is a parent who views themselves as autonomous and free to pass down that autonomy to their children. Infant baptism hits autonomy head-on, which is one reason many people have such a difficult struggle with it.

When I baptized my oldest son, God was declaring, "This is Andy. He is the first born of my redeemed servants, David and Patti. He belongs to me. The mark of baptism signifies this. Because of this mark he has an obligation to fulfill all of my covenant requirements, to trust and obey the God of his father and his mother." God made the same declaration when I baptized my daughter, Bethany, and my other son, Timothy. Since they have been marked out by God's covenant sign, I can hold each of them up as a child of the covenant. Just as God promised Abraham that he would have many descendants, as many as the grains of sand on the beach and the stars in the sky (Gen. 15:5; 22:17), and that all of these descendants would be his own property, so my children have become one of the heirs of God's promise to Abraham, one of the grains of sand on the beach, one of the stars in the sky. They belong to him, and to depart from covenant obedience to him would be to foolishly bring upon themselves all the covenant sanctions God imposes upon covenant breakers.

If the mark of God's ownership, namely baptism, has been put upon our children and they have been set apart for God's own holy use, then that means we have a responsibility to train them to acknowledge God's ownership and to live for his holy use (Deut. 6:1-25). God said of Abraham, "I have chosen him so that he may command his children and his household after him to keep the way of the Lord by doing righteousness and justice, so that the Lord may bring upon Abraham what he has spoken about him" (Gen. 18:19).

When our children are baptized, God is declaring his ownership and our stewardship. It is a sad commentary how many Christian parents are raising their children "to choose their own spiritual path" while submerged in a pagan world and pagan schools instructing them in a pagan lifestyle to make pagan decisions. The parents become distraught when their children don't respond with a godly, or at least a moral, lifestyle. The root of the frustration is in the failure to embrace what infant baptism declares: God owns us and our children and we must do things his way. Though God is not teaching that baptism regenerates our children, he is teaching that our children are not to be raised as pagans. They are to be raised as the children of God through the covenant community benefits of hearing the Word of God, prayer, experiencing the sacraments, and watching the example of redeemed living as they are constantly surrounded by those who acknowledge the one true Lord and worship him with all their heart, mind, soul, and strength. "How blessed is the man who does not walk in the counsel of the wicked, nor stand in the path of sinners, nor sit in the seat of scoffers! But his delight is in the law of the Lord, and in His law he meditates day and night. He will be like a tree firmly planted by streams of water, which yields its fruit in its season and its leaf does not wither; and in whatever he does, he prospers" (Ps. 1:1-3).

Benefit #5: To establish our children's citizenship in the covenant community

When a child is baptized in the midst of the congregation, the pastor performing the ceremony will usually ask the congregation whether or not they will undertake the responsibility of assisting the parents of the baptized child in his or her Christian nurture. Very few church members are ever unwilling to assist parents in the Christian nurture of their children. Why then is this question put to them as a solemn oath? It is to remind them that they have just received another member to their covenant community, obligating them to include this child in their community life and to take care of this child as one of their own. Where do these covenant community obligations come from?

First of all, let us consider the corporate nature of the people of God. God tells us that Jesus Christ "gave Himself for us to redeem us from every lawless deed and to purify for Himself *a people* for His own possession, zealous for good deeds" (Titus 2:14, emphasis added). This has nothing to do with us remaining as autonomous individuals. When God redeems us, individualism goes out the window. We become part of "a people."

Consider 1 Peter 2:9-10: "You are a chosen race, a royal priesthood, a holy nation, a people for God's own possession so that you may proclaim the excellencies of him who has called you out of darkness into his marvelous light; for you once were not a people but now you are the people of God. You had not received mercy but now you have received mercy." It is sad that we have allowed covenant theology—God's arrangement with Christ for his people—to lose its significance. It is difficult for us to see ourselves as more than a collection of individuals who have made the same choice to become Christians. Yet, the truth of Scripture is that we were not the ones making the choice. God made the choice, and he made us to be not a mere collection of individuals, but one people under his lordship. He has further commanded us in the Great Commission to go to every people group and to bring his children out of those groups and make them disciples under his lordship (Matt. 28:19-20).

Infant baptism establishes a child's entrance into the covenant community. It is one of those unique "family things" that God's family does that others may not do. It declares that "the Lord Himself is God; it is He who has made us, and not we ourselves; we are His people and the sheep of His pasture" (Ps. 100:3). Baptized children are not mere products of their environments. They are not the fruit of humanity, but they are God's creation and by the work of God in bringing them into this world through Christian parents they are being marked out as covenant community members (Gen. 17:6-13).

Citizenship in the covenant community is extremely important since it is here where the Holy Spirit is especially at work to draw people to Christ. It is "the church of God which He purchased with His own blood" (Acts 20:28). It is to the church that those who are saved are added on a daily basis (Acts 2:47). God has never been interested in taking a collection of individual strangers and foreigners to heaven, but rather he wants to take "fellow citizens with the saints," those who are of the household of God (Eph. 2:19). Gaining entrance into the covenant community is a high privilege regardless of the level of entrance. Apart from the work of the Holy Spirit in this community, salvation does not ordinarily occur.

Isn't it marvelous and wonderful that God would want our sons and daughters to be included in the covenant community as fellow citizens? Since this is true, there are obligations for us in the way we treat our children. Consider Ezekiel 16:20-21. In this passage, God rebukes his church from misusing *his children*. Those children, who have been marked out as fellow citizens of the kingdom of God, are considered by God to be his children. In 1 Corinthians 7:14, God calls them his holy ones. Their parents are obligated to train them up in the nurture and admonition of the Lord (Eph. 6:1-4), and parents will be held accountable for this task. Yet, the parents need assistance. No member of their covenant community has ever been expected to perform all of their responsibilities in isolation. Each one of us has been given "the manifestation of the Spirit for the common good" (1 Cor. 12:7).

We are to build one another up, exhorting, instructing, rebuking, and admonishing one another until we all become fully mature as the body of Christ (Eph. 4:11-16). When a child is baptized, we must do more than merely pray for that child's salvation. We must assist the parents by encouraging them through the Word of God, sharing the wisdom God teaches us. We must support them through the difficult moments of godly discipline. We must set before these fellow citizens of the covenant examples of good covenant citizenship. When their parents instruct them to love the Lord their God with all their heart, mind, soul, and strength, we must show them examples of holy zeal in worshiping God. When their parents instruct them to study God's Word and to become devoted to it, we must provide those children examples of serious students of the Scripture who have no need to be ashamed.

Infant baptism establishes citizenship, and we who are members of that covenant community need to take that citizenship seriously. We also need to worship our God with gratefulness for the privilege of being made citizens of his kingdom. The privilege of citizenship is "…for you and your children and for all who are far off, as many as the Lord our God will call to Himself" (Acts 2:39). God has made the call to us to be citizens of his eternal kingdom. To him be the glory.

Benefit # 6: To receive help with godly correction and compassionate evangelism

God not only wants us to go into all the world and make disciples, he expressly wants us to go into our families and make disciples. If we are believers, we are his instruments of redeeming love to our families. His desire is to sanctify our entire household (1 Cor. 7:14). Understanding that God wants to see our children converted, let us realize that the message of salvation in Christ is communicated not only through the Word of God, but also through the sacraments of Christ. The sign of baptism is one of God's special revelations. It accompanies his Word as a special tool given to parents to lead their children to repentance and faith in Christ. Our children need to know that God has not only written down his revelation for us, which leads us to Christ, but in baptism he has given us a visible sermon of his work to cleanse us from all of our sin and to unite us to himself as one purified people.

"We love, because He first loved us" (1 John 4:19). We were not born with the ability to love God; we love him because he first loved us. We were born depraved in sin and with no desire to embrace our God and his ways. We were born in love with ourselves, acting hostile towards anyone, including God, who would deny us our autonomy. The reason we have any love for God at all is because he has given us a new heart, a new record, a new life, and a new ability to please him. In baptism, he presents a picture of his condescension from heaven to provide us with this new, clean, holy existence.

A similar symbol is found in our culture in a marriage engagement ring. When it is given to a young lady, it is a visible expression that the giver desires her immediate response to his proposal of marriage. When baptism is administered to a child, a visible expression is given to that child that God desires a response to his covenantal marriage agreement. It is a sign that God has made the first move. He has loved that child first. The child is now obligated to respond to God's love through repentance and faith, calling upon Jesus Christ to be his Lord and Savior. If the child disrespectfully refuses to respond to God's love, they are marked out by God as a covenant breaker. Baptism thus becomes a tool that cries for an urgent response to God's grace. We should never neglect reminding our children of God's Word and of his visible sermon to be engaged to them through their faith and repentance in Christ. Remember the words of Exodus 19:5-6.

> Now then, if you will indeed obey My voice and keep My covenant, then you shall be My own possession among all the peoples, for all the earth is Mine; and you shall be to Me a kingdom of priests and a holy nation. These are the words that you shall speak to the sons of Israel.

God obligates us and our children to respond to his covenant through obedience. And though we have received the sign of his covenant, we will clearly receive his wrath if we do not keep it (Ps. 78:10-72). In other words, covenant participants who despise the covenant are under much stricter judgment than the pagans outside the covenant community who have never been marked out by God. We should tremble at every baptism if we do not take our covenant obligations seriously. For then we are heaping condemnation upon ourselves and upon our children.

As we seek to train up our children in the ways of the Lord, we need to communicate to them the wonderful manner in which God has already shown his love to them. We need to explain how God has loved them first, how God has initiated a covenant relationship with them. We need to explain the mark that God has placed on them through baptism, and that now as a baptized covenant citizen they are obligated to repent and believe. Their responsibility is to see that their life consistently points in the same direction as their baptismal sign, and that is to the reception of Christ and his righteousness. We do our children a disservice when we ignore their status as covenant citizens. They feel the weight of God's claim on their lives and seek to suppress it (Rom. 1:18), but we should not allow our children to inhibit God's work. We must remind them when others are baptized that they too have received God's mark upon their life. Whenever they disobey or misbehave we need to take hold of them by their baptism and exhort them to live consistently with it. They are under the obligations of God's covenant, and God has placed us in authority over them to train them in their covenant obligations, compassionately lead them to Christ, and correct them when they go astray. The tool of baptism is a great means for the work of godly training, correction, and evangelizing our children.

When my children began driving cars, there were about five hundred people in our local church. I told them that if they ever drove too fast, there were five hundred pairs of eyes watching, and I would be told. And I was. This is called baptism accountability. With baptism comes the rich resource of the whole body of Christ to encourage and admonish us to live as covenant community members. When our children went astray, we would yank them back through the loving prayers and admonition of our church and the enablement of the Holy Spirit. We told them they were not being raised to live as they pleased. God had already marked them out to be his, and they were required to live like it.

Christ is Lord and we are not. He calls the shots, he directs our paths. It is for us to be submissive servants. We have been bought with a price! Many times our children heard this message, and what a glory it was to see them one by one surrender to his grace, turn from their sin, and embrace Jesus as their Lord and Savior! Baptism places our children and our church in a position to understand the good news of Christ and to embrace it by faith. How blessed we are when we are regularly placed in a position to rightly hear the truth of God! "Faith comes from hearing, and hearing by the word of Christ" (Rom. 10:17).

Jesus Christ is the one who saves sinners, not baptism. Therefore, to those of us who are parents of children to be baptized, we are exhorted not to rely on our own dedication, or on our giving of our children in some ceremonial fashion to Christ for their redemption. They will not be saved through rituals or patterns. They must be saved by the Holy Spirit who regenerates them through the works of Christ. God tells us in 1 Corinthians 7:14 that he chooses to use believing parents to sanctify children and to make them holy. We should therefore begin each day asking the Lord to let this be the day we finally communicate the truth of Christ clearly to our children. We should begin each day asking the Lord to let this be the day he responds to our prayers and sends the Holy Spirit to regenerate our child and to reconcile him or her to God through Christ Jesus. We should begin each day asking the Lord to let this be the day that our child comes to us and says, "Mommy and Daddy, I love the Lord Jesus and I will love him for the rest of my life." We need to make it clear to our children that though we have baptized them and marked them out to be the Lord's, they are in need of turning from their sins, believing on the Lord Jesus Christ as their Lord and Savior, and keeping his commands throughout their days.

It is the customary procedure of lumber companies to mark out certain trees in a forest that they want to save. They then go into a forest and cut everything else. In the same way, baptism is a ritual or custom given to us by God in which we mark out the ones we want to see God save. Let your children know they have been marked out for salvation and need to embrace Christ. For if they have been marked out to be saved, and then they reject Christ, their life would be worse than had they never been born.

God promises in Psalm 112:1-2 that those parents who fear the Lord and greatly delight in his commands will have descendants that are mighty on the earth. Plead with God on a daily basis that he will not forsake the work of his hands, that he will use you as parents to bring your children to faith in Christ by his grace. Make sure you live a consistent life of faith in Christ and obedience to his commands before them. God desires both your salvation and your children's. The promise God gives us in Acts 16:31 is this, "Believe in the Lord Jesus, and you will be saved, you and your household."

Benefit # 7: To promote the covenant life of great joy and glory in Christ

It brings a parent great joy when their children mature to the place of appreciation for the parenting they have received. The vows my wife and I, along with our church family, were asked and affirmed at the baptism of our three children were as follows:

Parental Baptism Vows

1. Do you acknowledge your child's need of the cleansing blood of Jesus Christ, and the renewing grace of the Holy Spirit?
2. Do you claim God's covenant promises in his behalf, and do you look in faith to the Lord Jesus Christ for his salvation, as you do for your own?
3. Do you now unreservedly bring your child to God to be marked out as a covenant child, and promise in humble reliance upon divine grace, that you will endeavor to set before him a godly example, that you will pray with and for him, that you will teach him the doctrines of Scripture, and that you will strive by all the means of God's appointment to bring him up in the nurture and admonition of the Lord?

Congregational Baptism Vow

> Do you as a congregation undertake the responsibility of assisting the parents in the Christian nurture of this child?

My children hear these words today and rejoice. They give glory to God for being raised in a family where their salvation was always a central issue and where total dependence upon God and his grace for repentance, faith, and holiness was always the need. We are together thankful and give glory to God for fellow believers who have surrounded us with prayers and biblical admonition to live as faithful members of the body of Christ. We look upon our infant baptisms with great gratitude, not only because it provided our early admission into the visible body of Christ with all the benefits, but also because it was a prevailing tool for the revelation of God's saving love for us and our need for him. The good work that God continues to do through our lives can never be divorced from the influence of his Spirit through our baptism.

My father sold some property and determined to take all of the proceeds from that sale and establish college savings plans for all of his grandchildren. What a blessing! We never look upon my Dad's decision to invest in our children's education as something of no benefit because the children were too young to understand the ceremony or the legal paperwork involved. To the contrary, we all are grateful for great provisions. In the same way, our children did not understand the ceremony or the prayers and vows of their infant baptism at the time of the baptism, but there is much joy that follows, and all to the glory of God.

Not only is there joy through baptism for those baptized and for their parents, but there is also much joy for the church members who get the privilege of being participants in the baptism ceremony. They get to see the sign and seal that God puts before them. The sign of the need for God to come down from above to rest upon us in the power and person of his Spirit, the sign of his cleansing grace washing all our sins away, of our union to Christ, of our need for faith, repentance, and holiness, of God's willingness to love sinners who can do nothing good for themselves, and to provide us with all glory and honor and raise us up with Christ. As the church begins to see and meditate upon all that God pictures and promises us in baptism, she begins to worship in spirit and truth. We may clap our hands to encourage obedience in parents and children, but we humbly and joyfully bow before our God and lift our highest praises to him for a grace that covers all our sin.

To claim that infant baptism makes no difference is to be badly informed regarding this divine means of grace. Saying baptism doesn't do anyone any good is failing to understand it and employ it as God intended. Let us be careful to avoid corrupt ideas concerning infant baptism so we can enjoy its comforts.

Many parents today feel defeated at rearing their children in a godly fashion. Many times the reason for this is that they simply fail to approach the task in the right frame of mind. They fail to rear their children rooted in the promises of God. When we forget God's promises, we are right to feel defeated. The practice of infant baptism is one of God's visual reminders of glorious victory and comfort for parents, and also for the entire church family regarding their youngest covenant citizens.

Infant baptism reminds us that our children are included in the covenant and they are recipients of its promises. Infant baptism reminds us that God has not rejected our children, but that he looks upon them as his peculiar people. He is more concerned about our children than we are, and he is not wringing his hands, wondering what he is going to do about their disobedience. Christ already bids them to come to him, for the kingdom of God belongs to them. We need to accept God's infant baptism benefits and enjoy his smile on us as obedient children, to know more completely his love, and to declare more clearly his ownership for our stewardship. We also need apply the benefits of infant baptism to establish our children's citizenship in the covenant community, receive help with their godly correction and evangelism, and promote the covenant life of great joy and glory we have in Christ.

If the blessings and encouragements of infant baptism are so rich and wonderful, why then do not all Christian parents have their children baptized? In the old covenant, it would have been foolish to restrain one's infant son from the covenant sign of circumcision. Those who didn't have this sign were declared covenant breakers and cut off from the people of God. "But an uncircumcised male who is not circumcised in the flesh of his foreskin, that person shall be cut off from his people; he has broken My covenant" (Gen. 17:14). Covenant blessings were celebrated in the covenant sign and they were not neglected.

"And when eight days had passed, before His circumcision, His name was then called Jesus, the name given by the angel before He was conceived in the womb" (Luke 2:21). Jesus was circumcised when he was born, and when he was crucified, all four gospels tell us his garments were gambled away, leaving Christ naked. As both Jews and Gentiles looked at the crucified Christ, they could see the sign of the covenant; they could see the circumcised seed of Abraham; they could see the sign of the promise of redemption of the world. The sign had been fulfilled; Jesus was Immanuel, God in the flesh. The good news was proclaimed that Christ has become our circumcision through the outward sign of baptism (Col. 2:10-12).

Under the old, weaker covenant, circumcision was for Abraham and his seed—and as many as were far off and called to be God's people by grace. Under the new and better covenant, what restrains us as heirs of Abraham from applying the new and better sign of the circumcision of water through Jesus Christ to our infant children? Let us inform our children that they are heirs of the covenant with God, and let us raise them as such, all the while pleading for the tender mercies of Christ to be applied through the work of his Spirit. Does God find us with faith for these things?

"By faith Noah, being warned by God about things not yet seen, in reverence prepared an ark for the salvation of his household, by which he condemned the world, and became an heir of the righteousness which is according to faith" (Heb. 11:7). This benefit of being an heir of the righteousness of God came to Noah and his household when he was the only one to believe. By faith, Abraham lived with his sons Isaac and Jacob in a foreign land, and they became fellow heirs of the promise of God with him: "Abraham ...obeyed by going out to a place which he was to receive for an inheritance; and he went out, not knowing where he was going. By faith he lived as an alien in the land of promise, as in a foreign land, dwelling in tents with Isaac and Jacob, fellow heirs of the same promise" (Heb. 11:8-9). By faith, the mother Sarah and her children not yet born became as numerous "as the stars of heaven in number, and innumerable as the sand which is by the seashore" (Heb. 11:11-12).

By faith, Moses was protected as a child; he kept the Passover and the sprinkling of the blood and was spared the slaughter which came upon the Egyptians when they tried to pass through the Red Sea (Heb. 11:23-29). By faith, a mother named Rahab saw her whole household spared from destruction (Heb. 11:30-31), and by faith, Jairus' daughter was resurrected (Matt. 9:18-19; 23-26). By faith, the father of an epileptic son saw his son healed (Matt. 17:14-18), and by faith, Zaccheus was saved and salvation came to his whole household (Luke 19:9). By faith, a royal official saw his son healed from near death (John 4:46-54). How many examples do we need of godly parents and church members exercising faith for the benefit of their children and larger church family? Let us claim God's covenant promises and love for our children, and let us allow the children of the saints to be baptized. Why would we want God to return and find us without faith?

> They will not labor in vain, or bear children for calamity; for they are the offspring of those blessed by the Lord, and their descendants with them.
>
> —Isa. 65:23

Discussion and Study Questions

1. What is the faith element required in Bible reading or baptism, and how does someone go about obtaining it?
2. "To understand baptism's significance and to receive its rich blessings, the focus must always be on divine graciousness not human responsiveness?" Do you agree? How does one go about shifting their focus from man to God?

3. Which views corrupt the biblical doctrine of infant baptism and lead us away from its rich rewards?
4. Christian parents will rightly discuss with their believing children potential abuses of the Lord's Supper. Less frequently do they discuss the potential abuses of baptism. Why is this the case, and what can be done to improve this situation?
5. In 1 Corinthians 7:14, God declares that the unsaved children of believing parents are not to be reckoned as part of the world but rather as part of the church. Our children are not to be treated as pagans waiting to choose a god. When believing parents understand this, how does it impact their child-rearing?
6. How is it a kindness of God to view our children differently than the rest of the children in the world who do not belong to believing parents?
7. How does infant baptism establish a child's entrance into the covenant community? What are the ramifications of this for the entire covenant community—and the world?
8. As we seek to train up our children in the ways of the Lord, what are some of the things we need to communicate regarding the love of God? How does baptism picture these things for our children and for us all?
9. How can a family structure their lives so that salvation by Christ is always a central issue, and that total dependence upon God and his grace for repentance, faith, and holiness is always the need? How does baptism serve as a helpful tool and constant means of joy for this?
10. The practice of infant baptism is one of God's visual reminders of glorious victory and comfort for parents and the entire church family regarding their youngest covenant citizens. What will it take for parents to learn to rear their children in the victory and joy of being rooted in the promises of God?

Chapter 8

Examining the Validity of Our Baptisms

A COLLEGE STUDENT came to me with doubts about the validity of her baptism. We examined her life biblically and confidently concluded that she had been genuinely saved from the bondage of sin and the wrath of God by the sovereign mercy of God. She had been baptized while an infant and her mother was a Christian at that time. However, while at college, this student began attending a church that regarded her childhood baptism as invalid. They urged her to be rebaptized, claiming that in reality it would be her first and only "real baptism." Before being baptized the second time, she asked for my counsel. Since I was her pastor, it seemed fitting to her that if she needed to be baptized, whether for the first time or for another time, she should have the sacrament performed in her home church. The main question, however, was did she need another baptism? Was her first baptism a non-baptism, or was it good enough?

The act of rebaptism is based on the assumption that there is some inadequacy or deficiency in the previous baptism. I had a good friend tell me he believed in infant baptism, but planned to have his children rebaptized upon their profession of faith in Christ. Why would someone want to do this if they truly understood the sufficiency of infant baptism properly administered? His confusion was over what baptism points to. He wanted it to point to his child's own individual faith. But baptism was not designed by God as a sign of anyone's faith. Rather, it is a sign of God loving us before we loved him, making a covenant with us to be our God, and choosing us as his people.

Many people wonder whether or not their baptism is undeniably a valid biblical baptism. Suppose someone was presented for baptism by non-Christian parents when they were a child. Have they had a valid baptism? Suppose someone was presented for baptism as a child, but the preacher called it a christening service or dedication service. Was it a valid baptism? Suppose someone was presented for baptism as a converted adult, and yet later he or she determined they were deceived and were without real saving faith at the time of their baptism. Did they receive authentic Christian baptism? Some people were baptized in a church and later discovered the preacher who baptized them was not a Christian. Is their baptism valid? If a church is baptizing an individual with water in the name of the Father, Son, and the Holy Spirit as a sign and seal of the covenant of grace and engrafting into Christ, is the baptism still real even if the person being baptized has not yet been saved? Suppose water and the Trinitarian formula is used, but the church is apostate. Would baptism in such a place still be a good baptism?

In one of the fastest growing megachurches of our land, the pastor asked those attending on a particular Sunday morning to raise their hands if they had been baptized by sprinkling or as an infant. After a multitude of hands were raised, he proceeded to tell them that any baptism by sprinkling or any baptism performed while an infant was invalid, since it did not present the picture of being buried with Christ as found in Romans 6. He then encouraged all of those baptized wrongly to turn from their wrong baptisms that day and be immediately baptized by him and his staff by immersion. Only after such a baptism could they be counted as true believers (and for his records, "new believers") and members of the church. Many believers, unaccustomed to examining preachers and their messages through reading the whole revelation of God daily (Acts 17:11), were deceived, and others were greatly distressed by his example of counting "old believers" as "new believers" and dismissing valid baptisms as though they were invalid.

What constitutes a valid baptism? Let us consider criteria by which to judge a baptism's validity with the hope of being like-minded regarding "one baptism" and exhibiting much love and unity in the body of Christ.

Criteria for Examining Baptisms

Since baptism is a sign of God's covenant union with his people given to his church by the Lord Jesus Christ (Matt. 28:19-20; Acts 2:41-42; 1 Cor. 12:13), it would make sense that it could be invalidated either by anyone who does not represent the true church of Christ, or who performs a baptism as though it were a baptism of the true church but who administers it in a wrong manner. From this I suggest five questions to assist our evaluation process.

Evaluating Baptisms

1. Was it a "true church" baptism?
2. Was it a baptism "into" Christ in the name of the triune God?
3. Was it performed with water?
4. Was it designed for professing Christians or their children?
5. Was it administered under Christ's authority?

Was it administered by a true church of Christ? (Matt. 28:19; Acts 2:38)

For our purposes, a *true church* will be defined as one that proclaims the truth of the gospel of Christ. Thus, even if everything about baptism is performed correctly but it is done where the gospel of Christ is not proclaimed, it is not a valid baptism. A valid baptism can only take place within a true branch of the church of Jesus Christ. The sacrament of baptism was given by Christ to be administered by the church within its ministry. He said, "Go therefore and make disciples of all the nations, baptizing them in the name of the Father and the Son and the Holy Spirit" (Matt. 28:19). God's people alone are those who are to go and do the baptizing. Those who are not the people of God, not living and proclaiming the good news of Christ, cannot be baptizing for Christ and into Christ.

For example, the ministry of baptism has not been given by God to an institution or group like the Unitarians, Mormons, or Jehovah Witnesses, even though they are all known to perform baptisms. They may claim to be Christian, but they do not represent the true church of Christ; their message is a distortion of the gospel and they are accursed by God (Gal. 1:6-9). The apostle Paul proclaims that those who embrace the doctrine of false teachers will find it to be of "no benefit" (Gal. 5:2). Those who are severed from Christ and offer no benefit from Christ cannot perform the sacraments of Christ with validity, and this is true even if they try to do so with water and a Trinitarian formula. As to the Roman Catholic Church, there is significant debate concerning how far they have proceeded into apostasy. Some Christians are convinced the Roman Catholics have repudiated the gospel of grace alone through faith alone, and that this would invalidate them as a true church—thus invalidating their message and their sacraments. Anyone seeking to be justified by the law is clearly severed from Christ and fallen from grace (Gal. 5:4), and their baptism is not a baptism of grace but a work of man for merit. This is not a valid baptism. Converts to Christ from the groups just mentioned should be given instruction in this matter and offered true Christian baptism.

It should also be said that just as the ministry of baptism was not given to false churches or false teachers, its judgment for validity was not given to individuals apart from the organized true church of Jesus Christ. Oversight of the church and its sacraments is given to the elders of the church (Acts 20:28; 1 Pet. 5:1-2; Heb. 13:17). Thus the validity of baptism should not be left to the judgment of individuals, but should be decided by the elders of the church.

If baptism is administered in a church that denies the gospel of Christ by grace, then its baptism should be considered invalid.

However, if baptism is administered in a church that does not deny the gospel, then we should be very cautious in invalidating the baptism, since it would be assumed that the baptism is a baptism into Christ with water requiring faith and under biblical authority. The misguided works of a true church might obscure the biblical message of baptism, but it need not invalidate it. The circumcision performed by the unordained Zipporah was treated as valid, even though at best it was highly irregular (Exod. 4:24-26).

Was it a baptism into Christ in the name of the Triune God? (Matt. 28:19; Acts 2:38)

When Christ instituted the sacrament of baptism along with his Great Commission, he specifically decreed that baptism should be performed in the name of God the Father, God the Son, and God the Holy Spirit.

> Go therefore and make disciples of all the nations, baptizing them in the name of the Father and the Son and the Holy Spirit.
>
> —Matt. 28:19

The only exception to this rule is found in Acts 2:38:

> Peter said to them, "Repent, and each of you *be baptized in the name of Jesus Christ* for the forgiveness of your sins; and you will receive the gift of the Holy Spirit.
>
> —emphasis added

This passage of Scripture indicates baptism would be valid if it was simply in the name of Jesus Christ. These baptisms are not different since Christ is the mediatorial representative of the Trinity (1 Tim. 2:5; Heb. 8:6; 9:15; 12:24). In other words, through Christ all of the Godhead is involved. Baptism is thus invalid whenever a non-Trinitarian view of God is embraced as the object of faith. Such a baptism would simply not be what Christ has instituted, and thus it would be without biblical support.

Was it performed with water, whether by sprinkling, pouring, or immersion? (Matt. 3:11, John 1:33)

All biblical baptisms include the element of water as a symbol of cleansing from sin through covenantal union with the Father, Son, and Holy Spirit through the pouring out of the Spirit on the one being baptized. I have never heard of anyone disputing the necessity of water as the ingredient required for a valid baptism, but as soon as we neglect to state it, someone will want to use sand or blood or some other substance.

Since the manner of water (mode of baptism) is not revealed as essential to baptism's effectiveness, immersionists should allow for sprinkling, just as those who sprinkle should allow for full immersion. And we both must dwell together in unity. This does not mean we should abandon our scriptural convictions about the matter, or cease examining these things. We only reach perfect unity when we reach it doctrinally (John 17:17-21). But it should be unheard of that any division exists among us because of water baptism. We are one body in Christ and there is but one baptism (Eph. 4:5). Whether we sprinkle or immerse, we have one Lord, one faith, and one baptism signifying union with Christ through the outpouring of the Holy Spirit in the name of the Father, Son, and Holy Spirit.

Nevertheless, a problem exists within the church for those who will not accept baptism by sprinkling or pouring. They either reject the chosen of God whom Christ has purchased with his own blood, or if they do admit them to the Lord's Table and church membership, they still treat them as second class believers, as those who walk in perpetual failure to submit to coming under their baptism water. Such unbiblical treatment of the saints of God can only be maintained through adding to the Word of God—teaching as doctrines the precepts of men (Matt. 15:3-9).

One of the men God graciously brought to faith in Christ under my ministry was transferred with his job promotion to a region of the country that had no strong Christ-centered church witness, except where immersion was required. My dear brother was not called to plant a new local church, so he chose to admonish the pastor and elders of the church near him to find him genuinely converted to Christ through faith and repentance, and his spiritual gifts granted by God's grace and given for the common good of the body of Christ (1 Cor. 12:7). How could they refuse him church membership and the full use of his gifts among his brothers and sisters in the faith because he did not embrace their view on immersion? They told him that the sixth chapter of Romans requires immersion. He said that was not so. Since Scripture interprets Scripture, and since the overwhelming majority of the texts of Scripture clearly picture baptism by sprinkling and pouring, then sprinkling and pouring was as an established practice long before Romans 6 was written. He said that Romans chapter six therefore cannot be the definitive passage. This church changed their local bylaws to allow sprinkling and pouring along with immersion as acceptable modes for baptism, and now the brothers and sisters dwell together in unity.

Most paedobaptists (those who sprinkle and pour in infant baptism) accept the church membership of one who has been immersed, and we need to pray this will be true the other way around. The path to unity is to realize that the essence of baptism practice is the use of water in the name of the triune God by an ordained church minister with the intent of those involved being that of participating in a Christian baptism. The manner in which the water is applied (immersion, sprinkling, or pouring) certainly matters, but it does not invalidate the baptism. "Is not the cup of blessing which we bless a sharing in the blood of Christ? Is not the bread which we break a sharing in the body of Christ? Since there is one bread, we who are many are one body; for we all partake of the one bread" (1 Cor. 10:16-17).

Was it designed for professing Christians, or for their children? (Gen. 17:7-9; Mark. 16:15-16; Acts 2:38-42; 8:37-38; 1 Cor. 7:14)

Baptism is for those who profess faith in Christ and their children. In other words, its design should be a "Christian covenantal baptism." It is for everyone who participates through faith in the covenant of God as the people of God. This criterion of a valid baptism focuses on the fact that those requesting baptism and those performing baptism must have as their intent and motive that of participating in a distinctly Christian baptism. Regardless of the depth of their knowledge about the biblical doctrine of baptism, their intent must be that of fulfilling the obligations of the new covenant and Great Commission of Christ. This clearly distinguishes a valid baptism from a non-Christian christening service or mere dedication service for one's self or one's child. In the case of infant baptisms, parents would say that they were doing what they were doing for God and not for themselves—because God requires it and not just because they wanted a cute religious moment for their scrapbook.

As far as the covenant of grace is concerned, God requires those who have entered into this covenant to be marked out as covenant members through baptism (Acts 2:38-42; Mark 16:15-16). If believers have children, the covenant of grace requires that they also mark out their children as members of the covenant of grace by the sacrament of baptism (Gen. 17:7-9; Col. 2:11-12). In order to have one's child baptized, a credible profession of faith in Christ must be given to the elders of the church (Acts 2:38-42; 8:37-38). The absolute infallible certainty of one's regeneration cannot be required for a valid baptism. What is required is a credible profession of faith in Christ. The intention of a true profession of faith in Christ must be present, though the reality of it may indeed be lacking.

Was it administered under Christ's authority by a minister of the gospel? (1 Cor. 4:1; 11:23; Heb. 5:4)

There are no examples in Scripture of baptism being performed by anyone other than one specifically called to the task by God. Since baptism is a sacrament given specifically by Christ to the church, then it must come under the authority of the elders who have been commissioned to guard the church and oversee it (Acts 20:28). The elders of the church are to see that the sacrament of baptism is in no way profaned. The example in Scripture is that only a lawfully called elder or minister of the gospel is to administer the sacrament of baptism.

Criteria Not Needed to Make Baptism Good Enough

Regeneration by the candidate for baptism

Baptism begins with faith, the faith of the baptism candidate or his parent, and faith in Christ is a fruit of regeneration. The presence of faith, however, does not guarantee the genuineness of the faith. There are times when faith in Christ is lacking regeneration of the heart and this can't be known by simply asking about it. Even those who express faith in Christ, which later turns out to be a false faith, have no idea they are lacking regeneration. They are deceived. Many are deceived even on the great last day of judgment, convinced they have sufficiently believed in Jesus and have lived for him, yet Christ still declares "I never knew you; depart from me" (Matt. 7:15-23).

> As a result of this many of His disciples withdrew and were not walking with Him anymore. So Jesus said to the twelve, "You do not want to go away also, do you?" Simon Peter answered Him, "Lord, to whom shall we go? You have words of eternal life. We have believed and have come to know that You are the Holy One of God." Jesus answered them, "Did I Myself not choose you, the twelve, and yet one of you is a devil?" Now He meant Judas the son of Simon Iscariot, for he, one of the twelve, was going to betray Him.
>
> —John 6:66-71

In this passage, there were those who believed in Christ and were disciples of Christ who "withdrew and were not walking with him anymore." There is also the mention of Judas Iscariot, who definitely had faith in Christ that was so credible none of the other disciples knew he would betray Christ and prove to have false faith until his actual betrayal occurred. It is never mentioned that any of these baptized disciples (John 3:22-23) needed to improve their situation with another baptism. What they needed was regeneration evidenced through genuine faith and repentance.

> ...and all were baptized into Moses in the cloud and in the sea; and all ate the same spiritual food; and all drank the same spiritual drink, for they were drinking from a spiritual rock which followed them; and the rock was Christ. Nevertheless, with most of them God was not well-pleased; for they were laid low in the wilderness.
>
> —1 Cor. 10:2-5

This passage of Scripture indicates that *all* the children of Israel were baptized into Moses. Nevertheless, most of them were destroyed by God in the wilderness. The reason for this passage is to show us that we should not think our salvation is secured simply because we have gone through religious rituals or have inherited religious rituals. Baptism does not regenerate. We may have truly participated in many biblical privileges, yet still have not received eternal union with God. All the children of Israel received the outward sign of union with God, namely that of circumcision, having been baptized into Moses. They had all been obedient to God's Mosaic laws concerning his covenant of grace. Nevertheless, most of them were still lacking a regenerate heart. They were still unpleasing to God, and were destroyed by his righteous wrath.

There are many people in the church today who think that if they go through certain religious procedures in the right manner, then this will keep them safe and make them holy and acceptable to God. In the same way, many of the Israelites were baptized members of the covenant community, yet they were not among those who inherited the Promised Land. Instead, "they were laid low in the wilderness" (1 Cor. 10:5). Many people who are baptized today may not see the glories of heaven. They may have the sign of baptism, but they are without the regeneration of the heart and a saving union with Christ which baptism signifies.

Let it be clear that it is not unusual or out of the ordinary for many people in the church (the visible church) to receive the sacrament of baptism as an outward ritual yet still not be regenerate. When this is discerned to be the case, God does not teach us to wait for greater evidence of regeneration and then baptize another time. There are no examples of multiple baptisms because of this matter. We have already seen in the case of Simon the Sorcerer that he was told his need was for repentance from sin and not another baptism (Acts 8:9-24).

Regeneration, then, cannot be considered a requirement or criteria for a valid baptism. Genuine regeneration of the heart can only be known to our heart-searching God. It cannot be criteria for a valid baptism since God doesn't give the elders of the church or anyone else the means of infallible discernment in determining whether or not regeneration of the heart has indeed taken place. This does not mean that we should not require a credible profession of faith in Christ prior to baptism. All adults are to be baptized only after they repent and believe in Christ. The baptism of children is only to occur after a credible profession of faith from at least one of their parents.

A sacrament has two parts, the outward sensible sign and the inward spiritual grace. The name and effects of either one of these parts can be attributed to the other. It is only natural that there exists a close relationship between the sign and the thing signified. Therefore, the water (or ritual baptism) being the sign of baptism can be called baptism even when the thing signified (the reality of the Holy Spirit baptism) is lacking.

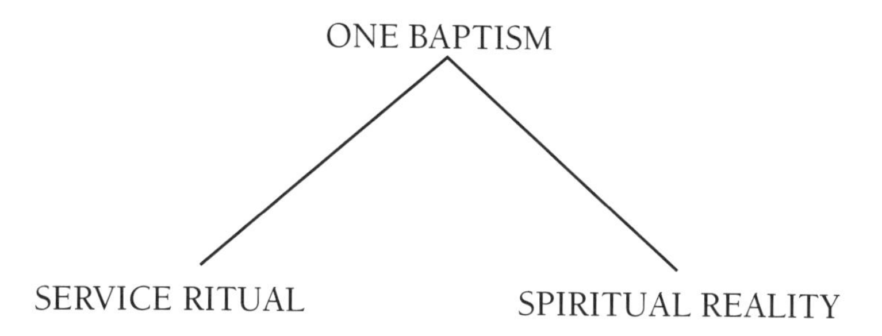

If a valid baptism is present only when the "thing signified" is genuinely present, then it denotes admission into the *invisible*

church rather than the *visible church*. In other words, if baptism is only good enough to remain when we can guarantee the person baptized was of the elect of God at the time of their baptism, and since baptism is a sign of one's inclusion into covenant community membership, then when we baptize someone, we are judging their faith and regeneration to be genuine and their admission into the church to be secure. God has not given men the omnipotence or omniscience necessary to admit someone into the invisible church. A profession of faith for visible church membership, not regeneration for invisible church membership, is sufficient to meet the requirement for a valid baptism.

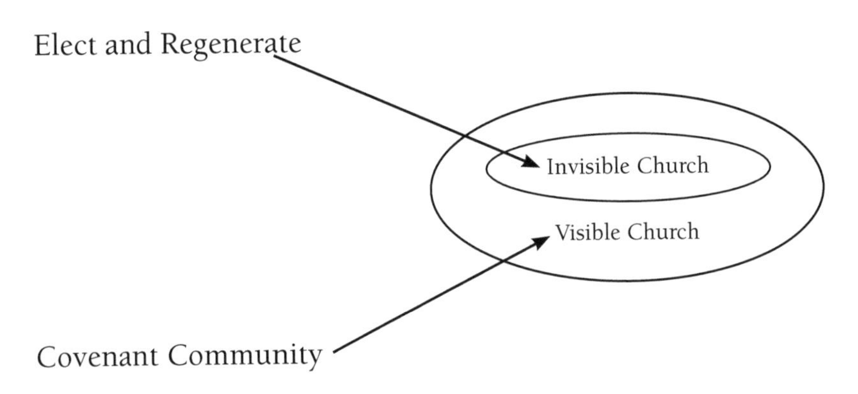

Genuine Holy Spirit baptism may either precede or follow ritual baptism in adults as well as in infants. Invisible church membership, granted through God's gracious election and regeneration, may either precede or follow visible church membership. The inward reality of baptism can only be said to be present when the recipient of baptism has truly been regenerated by the grace of God—something only God can know for sure. When regeneration is all that is lacking, baptism need not be repeated.

Suppose a simple road sign reads, "Mama's Restaurant Ahead." This sign is pointing us to Mama's Restaurant. When Mama's Restaurant burns to the ground, those who own it seek to salvage what they can and rebuild. But before they rebuild, there is a road sign that points to a restaurant that is not there. Do they need another sign after they rebuild? The sign is still a good sign doing all it needs to do as a sign. The need is not for a new sign, but only for rebuilding the restaurant. In the same way, baptism is a good sign pointing to our union with Christ. The sign could read, "Christian Ahead," in the case of an infant baptism, or it could read "You just passed a Christian," in the case of an adult baptism. In either case, if we later find out that we have no Christian at all, what we need is regeneration, not a new sign.

A proper understanding of baptism

> Therefore whoever eats the bread or drinks the cup of the Lord in an unworthy manner, shall be guilty of the body and the blood of the Lord. But a man must examine himself, and in so doing he is to eat of the bread and drink of the cup. For he who eats and drinks, eats and drinks judgment to himself if he does not judge the body rightly. For this reason many among you are weak and sick, and a number sleep. But if we judged ourselves rightly, we would not be judged. But when we are judged, we are disciplined by the Lord so that we will not be condemned along with the world.
>
> —1 Cor. 11:27-32

Though this passage of Scripture specifically deals with the sacrament of the Lord's Supper, it is relevant to the sacrament of baptism by way of analogy. What is true concerning the validity of one sacrament has implications for the validity of the other sacrament. As to the Lord's Supper, let us propose this question: "Can we say we have participated in and received benefit from the Lord's Supper, even if we have taken it wrongly?" The answer to this question has implications as to whether or not the sacrament of baptism has been truly received and benefited from, even if it were administered wrongly.

The admonitions and instructions regarding the Lord's Supper make sense precisely because it is a legitimate sacrament of the Lord, even if the people receiving it are receiving it wrongly. In Corinth, the Lord's Supper was being mishandled. Many were guilty of taking it "in an unworthy manner" and thus becoming "guilty of the body and the blood of the Lord"—even bringing judgment upon themselves. For these people, the sacrament ceased to be a means of grace and blessing and had become a means for judgment. Many had even become weak and sick, and some had died as a result of wrongly taking a sacrament which was valid and present among them. The Word of God comes to such people to admonish them to change their behavior by judging themselves in such a way that they begin to rightly handle the sacrament before them.

What does this imply for the sacrament of baptism? The Word of God teaches us that *an improper participation in a sacrament does not invalidate the sacrament.* It does preclude the sacrament's efficacy, but it does not make the sacrament null and void. In other words, it postpones the blessing of the sacrament and the grace of the sacrament, but it does not negate the reality of the sacrament in one's life.

Calling a baptism a christening or a dedication is wrongly handling the sacrament. Thinking that baptism was made to be a human-centered event applauding the exercise of personal faith in Christ, rather than worshiping God for his covenantal love for us and our children, misconstrues what baptism is. But mishandling and misunderstanding the sacrament does not invalidate it necessarily. Let us repent of all the times we have participated wrongly in the sacrament of baptism. Let us participate in it rightly from now on, every time it is before us. Let us capture its beauty and benefits for the glory and honor of our covenant-keeping Lord.

A timely administration of the baptism

> But when they believed Philip preaching the good news about the kingdom of God and the name of Jesus Christ, they were being baptized, men and women alike. Even Simon himself believed; and after being baptized, he continued on with Philip, and as he observed signs and great miracles taking place, he was constantly amazed. Now when the apostles in Jerusalem heard that Samaria had received the word of God, they sent them Peter and John, who came down and prayed for them that they might receive the Holy Spirit. For He had not yet fallen upon any of

> them; they had simply been baptized in the name of the Lord Jesus. Then they began laying their hands on them, and they were receiving the Holy Spirit. Now when Simon saw that the Spirit was bestowed through the laying on of the apostles' hands, he offered them money, saying, "Give this authority to me as well, so that everyone on whom I lay my hands may receive the Holy Spirit." But Peter said to him, "May your silver perish with you, because you thought you could obtain the gift of God with money! You have no part or portion in this matter, for your heart is not right before God. Therefore repent of this wickedness of yours, and pray the Lord that, if possible, the intention of your heart may be forgiven you. For I see that you are in the gall of bitterness and in the bondage of iniquity." But Simon answered and said, "Pray to the Lord for me yourselves, so that nothing of what you have said may come upon me."
>
> —Acts 8:12-24

Here we see that when some are baptized who have yet to be regenerated by God's grace, their need is *not* for a rebaptism because they were baptized at the wrong time. In this passage of Scripture, we read that Simon the sorcerer had believed the preaching of Philip and had been baptized. Simon believed in the Word of God to all appearance, just as everyone else did. No one seemed to have any doubts about Simon's profession of faith. Therefore, it was customary for him to proceed with the ritual of baptism along with the others. If Philip was deceived as to the true nature of Simon's faith and heart, then it only shows that he did not have the omniscient abilities of God in determining someone else's regenerate condition.

Later on, Peter uncovers Simon's true spiritual condition when he says, "Your heart is not right before God. Therefore repent of this wickedness of yours, and pray the Lord that, if possible, the intention of your heart may be forgiven you." It is possible at this point to presume that Simon only needed to repent of some specific sin. But when we read, "For I see that you are in the gall of bitterness and in the bondage of iniquity," we know his repentance needs to be a turning to God from self and bondage to sin. Simon was still in need of a conversion experience: a new heart, a new record, and a new life in Christ.

Notice that God's counsel to Simon through the apostle Peter was not that he needed to be rebaptized. Rather, God's counsel to Simon was that he needed to repent. Simon had already received the external water baptism, but he had yet to receive regeneration—the internal Spirit baptism. He had yet to receive genuine regeneration, repentance, and conversion to Christ. He had the symbol of baptism, but he did not have the reality of baptism. Had the external symbol of baptism been required to only take place after regeneration, God would have commanded Simon at this point to be rebaptized. However, since baptism was not required the second time, we must infer that baptism is but once to be administered per candidate. If a professing Christian desires at any time to in any way improve his baptism, the means for doing so is not a rebaptism, but rather repentance, more dying to sin and living to righteousness, which is the powerful life of freedom in Christ.

Though the practice of rebaptism is present in many churches today, there are no biblical passages showing anyone rightly baptized into Christ ever being rebaptized. There are no New Testament references to any covenant child receiving baptism as an adult. There are also no New Testament references of a baptized person who, having professed faith in Christ and then subsequently find himself to afterwards be truly converted, being rebaptized. The fact that Scripture lacks any references for Christian rebaptism should encourage us to likewise avoid rebaptism and support God's once-and-for-all covenant arrangement with his people. There is only "one baptism" (Eph. 4:5). Though God's people may have mishandled the sacrament, God has not mishandled it. What he has dispensed by his grace from heaven remains in force waiting the moment of our true regeneration. It is a man-invented and non-covenantal notion that man must contribute saving faith in order for his baptism to be a genuine baptism. The validity of a baptism does not rest upon man's faithfulness, but upon the covenant faithfulness of God.

Suppose you have been baptized by immersion, but now come to realize a more biblical position on baptism. What are you to do? You do not need another baptism. Recognize that many who were baptized in infancy are in the same place as you. Together you must learn what biblical baptism depicts and why it is so beautiful and beneficial. You need to see in baptism God's wonderful condescension to us by way of covenant, his promise to be our God, and to unite us to himself through the work of God the Father, God the Son, and God the Holy Spirit. He receives us by cleansing us from sin that we might be faithful to all the duties of the new covenant for us and our whole household.

Church Unity and Love

Hopefully, making careful and correct judgments regarding individual baptisms will let us return to loving those with whom we differ, especially those within the household of God. If the essential meaning and intent of a Christian baptism has not been left out of the ritual, if the baptism has occurred within a true branch of the church of Jesus Christ with Christ's authority, and if it has been administered to professing Christians or their children with water in the name of God the Father, Son, and Holy Spirit, we must practice an open church policy and not require rebaptism. We must not demand some additional local church standard, such as, "Be baptized our way or you will not be regarded as belonging to the obedient people of God." We must love and receive whom Christ has received into his church.

I was honored to be sought out as a counselor and consultant by a megachurch pastor in another city. After spending time together, he discovered some of my training tools for church elders. Although he was from a church tradition that did not recognize a plurality of elders in every local church as the ruling body of that church, he was convicted through the Word of God and the Holy Spirit that his church needed such men. I was then asked to provide the teaching and training his men needed to discern their calling as biblical elders. To make this story much shorter, I was asked to teach and train the officers and leaders in a church that would not let me join! I am accepted by Christ and a member in the universal invisible church of Christ, and yet I was barred from membership in the particular assembly of fellow saints I have been privileged to train for Christ. Why? Because I was baptized as an infant by sprinkling. Do we not see a problem with this?

God says, "Accept one another, just as Christ also accepted us to the glory of God" (Rom. 15:7). Differences in views on the ritual of baptism beyond the essential and necessary ingredients should not bar anyone from full communion in the body of Christ. We should not let water baptism be a wall of division among true believers in Christ. If we have one Lord and one faith, we should also have *one baptism* which signifies our union with our one Lord through faith.

Discussion and Study Questions

1. What issues or situations might arise that would cause one to evaluate the validity of their baptism? Why is it important that we be able to perform this evaluation in a biblical manner using biblical criteria? How might such an ability create unity in the church across denominational lines?
2. What do you think of the five questions used for evaluating the validity of baptisms? Do you want to add to or take away from these questions?
3. What should be done for those who were baptized in a Roman Catholic Church who then later join an evangelical Protestant church? Should they be rebaptized? Why or why not?
4. Since oversight of the church and its sacraments is given to the elders of the church (Acts 20:28; 1 Pet. 5:1-2; Heb. 13:17), should the validity of baptism rest with them, or should individuals themselves be able to determine whether their baptism is valid or not? If the church you join does not have elders, is baptism's validity then just an individual thing?

5. If the Trinitarian formula of being baptized in the name of the Father, Son, and Holy Spirit is essential for a valid baptism, what baptisms are then to be ruled invalid?
6. Since the manner of water (mode of baptism) is not revealed as essential to baptism's effectiveness, should immersionists allow for sprinkling and should those who sprinkle allow for full immersion? Would such action force believers to abandon their scriptural convictions about baptism?
7. Is it true or false that the infallible certainty of one's regeneration cannot be required for a valid baptism? Why or why not?
8. What criteria for the validity of baptisms might be proposed but is not necessary for the purpose of examining baptisms?
9. What is the difference between the wrong handling of baptism and an invalid baptism, and why is it important that we make this distinction?

Appendix

An Infant Baptism Service

Words of Direction and Instruction

WHAT A PRIVILEGE we have today of participating in the beauty and benefits of baptism. Let us all actively participate in obedience to the word of Christ. When a family has been given directions to a new restaurant, everyone who is hungry participates in finding it. Traveling down the road toward the restaurant, everyone is actively engaged in finding the signs that leads them to where they need to be. Let us be careful to look at the sign God has given that leads us to his covenant love for us.

> For the promise is for you and your children, and for all who are far off, as many as the Lord our God shall call to Himself.
>
> —Acts 2:39

> And I will establish My covenant between Me and you and your descendants after you throughout their generations for an everlasting covenant, to be God to you and to your descendants after you.
>
> —Gen. 17:7

> And they said, "Believe in the Lord Jesus, and you shall be saved, you and your household."
>
> —Acts 16:31

> "And as for Me, this is My covenant with them," says the Lord: "My Spirit which is upon you, and My words which I have put in your mouth, shall not depart from your mouth, nor from the mouth of your offspring, nor from the mouth of your offspring's offspring," says the Lord, "from now and forever."
>
> —Isa. 59:21

Baptism gives us a picture of our union with Christ through the work of the Holy Spirit coming down upon us to unite us with Christ, cleanse us from sin, and grant us adoption into God's family forever. We have seen from the Scriptures that the benefits coming with baptism have been given to those who, along with their children, profess faith in Christ.

When the child emerges from the waters of baptism, he or she is a different person—a baptized child! This means that the child has been changed. The child is not simply wet; he or she is baptized, and that makes a difference because God planned for it to make a difference. Just as God planned for the covenant of marriage to make a difference—applying enduring love to relationship difficulties making both husband and wife different (Mal. 2:14-16; 1 Cor. 13:4-8)—applying the waters of baptism makes a child different from those who have not yet been baptized. Being rightly baptized is such a significant action that it never needs repeating. It stands as a life-long sign of God's new covenant love and union with us. We should not downplay the specialness and beauty of what God has ordained.

By baptism, a child becomes a member of the visible church of Jesus Christ and is acknowledged as such. If the child were an American born in a foreign country, that child would be acknowledged as an American citizen and entitled to American government protection. But before his or her eighteenth birthday there must be a confirmation of this citizenship to continue this protection and benefits of being an American. A baptized child becomes a member of the visible church but is still in need of confirming membership through his own profession of faith in Christ to retain all the benefits of the covenant of grace.

A baptized child is the child of an obedient and dedicated parent who has received vows of nurture from an entire local church membership—what a blessing that is! This child will be raised to live for Christ and to make every decision for Christ. This child will be prayed for and prayed with. This child will be taught all of God's commands and have the weekly benefit of the Sabbath day and the proclamation of God's word in the power and presence of the Holy Spirit.

Baptism never guarantees salvation. No one is saved by their baptism. We are saved by God's grace alone through the work of Christ and the Holy Spirit received by faith, and even our faith is a gift of God so that none of us can claim any credit in our salvation. The glory goes to God alone. We pray for this work, that God will redeem those he has marked out through baptism. Just as a forester will mark trees he wants, we pray God will save those he has marked out through baptism. We pray for the gifts of faith and repentance that only God can provide, and we pray that baptism will be used as a tool to reveal the kindness of God towards sinners.

Prayer

Dear Father, through the help of the Holy Spirit we come before you seeking much grace and mercy. We acknowledge that none of us could have ever come to you on our own. As sinners, we were rightly cast from your holy presence. Yet you loved us so much, you came to us. You made a covenant with our father Abraham and with his seed who is Christ. You came to us in Christ. You made a new covenant with us in his blood. Let us see the sign of that covenant and give you the praise you deserve. In baptism, let us see the Holy Spirit poured out, and the blood of Christ sprinkled upon us for cleansing from sin. Let us see a God who loves us and our children, and let us worship you. Lord, we are without hope unless you come to us. Draw us to yourself. Let this family who comes for baptism be recipients of your grace. Let their child come to you for your blessing and be marked out as your covenant child. Grant them the strength to walk in full obedience before you and let them ever praise you and trust you that they would be saved, along with their whole household. To you be all glory, oh Lord, for we pray in Jesus name. Amen.

Parental Vows

1. Do you recognize that today's baptism does not save your child from sin or the judgment wrath of God, but that he needs to be sprinkled clean from sin with the blood of Christ through the work of the Holy Spirit, which is pictured in baptism?
2. Do you stand before God and his people today in obedience to the Word and the promises of God, trusting Christ Jesus alone for your salvation and earnestly seeking his saving grace for your child?
3. Do you then present your child to be baptized—marked out with water as a new covenant member—and promise that with all the strength God provides, you will train up your child in the way he should go, to make every decision for Christ through examining the Scriptures together, praying together, and loving the Lord your God together through weekly corporate worship?

Church Family Vow.

Do you, as fellow members of the same family of God, promise to love these who have come for baptism today, and to pray for them and support them by doing all you can to see this child living his whole life for Jesus?

Baptism

The minister, having prayed for God's blessing upon this baptism, shall say, "In obedience to God who commanded us to go to every ethnic group, make disciples, and baptize them, I baptize you in the name of the Father, and the Son, and the Holy Spirit. Amen."

Song of Response

"But the lovingkindness of the Lord is from everlasting to everlasting on those who fear Him, and His righteousness to children's children" (Ps. 103:17). Let us sing of this love.

Jesus loves me! This I know,
For the Bible tells me so.
Little ones to him belong;
They are weak, but he is strong.

Refrain:
Yes, Jesus loves me!
Yes, Jesus loves me!
Yes, Jesus loves me!
The Bible tells me so.

—Anna B. Warner, 1859

Made in the USA
Columbia, SC
28 December 2024